DATE DUE

Gus Gordon
Thurmon Williams

Doing Business in Mexico
A Practical Guide

Pre-publication
REVIEWS,
COMMENTARIES,
EVALUATIONS . . .

"This is a well-written, innovative book that focuses on the technical aspects of doing business in Mexico. It benefits from the expertise of Gus Gordon as an accountant and DBA and the experience of Thurmon Williams as former CEO and Chairman of the Board of Sears in Mexico. The book is an excellent source of valuable tips and is recommended for anyone interested in exploring new ventures in Mexico."

Dr. Francisco Carrada-Bravo
*Professor of World Business,
Thunderbird—The American Graduate
School of International Management,
Glendale, Arizona*

"*Doing Business in Mexico* presents a general overview of the benefits of investing in Mexico and provides basic information on issues such as taxation, importing and exporting, accounting, and laws regarding the establishment of a business in Mexico. It describes the advantages of doing business through the maquila program, thus reducing labor and transportation costs. The book gives investors, executives, and others the basic knowledge needed to plan and start business activities in Mexico. The language is clear and the examples simplify legal, tax, and business issues in a Mexican context."

Filio E. Alcaraz Mendoza, CPA
*Tax/Legal Partner,
KPMG Mexico,
Mérida*

Doing Business in Mexico
A Practical Guide

BEST BUSINESS BOOKS
Robert E. Stevens, PhD
David L. Loudon, PhD
Editors in Chief

Strategic Planning for Collegiate Athletics by Deborah A. Yow, R. Henry Migliore, William W. Bowden, Robert E. Stevens, and David L. Loudon

Church Wake-Up Call: A Ministries Management Approach That Is Purpose-Oriented and Inter-Generational in Outreach by William Benke and Le Etta N. Benke

Organizational Behavior by O. Jeff Harris and Sandra J. Hartman

Marketing Research: Text and Cases by Bruce Wrenn, Robert Stevens, and David Loudon

Doing Business in Mexico: A Practical Guide by Gus Gordon and Thurmon Williams

Doing Business in Mexico
A Practical Guide

Gus Gordon
Thurmon Williams

BEST BUSINESS BOOKS

Best Business Books®
An Imprint of The Haworth Press, Inc.
New York • London • Oxford

Published by

Best Business Books®, an imprint of The Haworth Press, Inc., 10 Alice Street, Binghamton, NY
13904-1580

Cover design by Jennifer M. Gaska.

Library of Congress Cataloging-in-Publication Data

Gordon, Gus, 1948-
    Doing business in Mexico : a practical guide / Gus Gordon, Thurmon Williams.
        p. cm.
    Includes bibliographical references and index.
    ISBN 0-7890-1213-8 (alk. paper)—ISBN 0-7890-1595-1 (alk. paper)
    1. Investments, Foreign—Mexico. 2. Business etiquette—Mexico. 3. Corporate culture—Mexico.
4. Mexico—Commerce. 5. Mexico—Commercial policy. 6. Corporations, American—Mexico. 7. International business enterprises—Mexico. I. Williams, Thurmon, 1937- II. Title.

HG5162 .G72 2001
658'.049'0972—dc21
                                                                            2001025796

CONTENTS

ABOUT THE AUTHORS

Gus Gordon, DBA, is a certified public accountant, a certified internal auditor, and has completed the ISO 9000 lead auditor certification course. He has published two books and over forty articles that have appeared in academic and professional journals. He has provided consulting to businesses in various industries, including maquiladoras, manufacturing, agribusiness, oil and gas, and service organizations. Dr. Gordon also holds the position of Associate Professor at the University of Southern Mississippi in Long Beach. Visit his Web site at <www.gusgordon.com>.

Thurmon Williams is the former CEO and Chairman of the Board of Sears de Mexico. During his six years with Sears de Mexico, he accomplished a remarkable turnaround of the company's fortunes. Besides Mexico, he has worked in South America, Central America, and Europe. He is currently on the operating board of a well-known investment firm, works as a consultant, and sits on several boards of directors in Mexico and South America.

Preface

This book is designed to assist entrepreneurs, managers, and investors who are considering doing business in Mexico. The purpose of the book is not to make one an expert, but to educate one about the basics of doing business in Mexico. We believe that the knowledge imparted by the book will enable the achievement of two important objectives: (1) to provide the tools to evaluate business opportunities in Mexico and to know what questions to ask in the evaluation process, and (2) to provide the knowledge to operate a business in Mexico fully cognizant of the risks, threats, and opportunities posed by doing business there.

Our approach is to educate from a technical and cultural perspective. Although the technical aspects—the legal, tax, and accounting aspects—of doing business in Mexico appear to be very similar to those in the U.S. system, they are not. Culturally, business and social protocol are very important in Mexico and quite different from the U.S. business culture. We discuss both the technical and cultural aspects from a practical perspective, providing examples and tips to illustrate important points.

The practical elements of the book, we think, set it apart from others. Further, our different business experiences, from which the practical examples and tips are drawn, are complementary. One of us was the chief executive officer (CEO) and chairman of the board of a multibillion-dollar company headquartered in Mexico City and continues to consult with large companies. The other author consults primarily with small companies and entrepreneurs. The result, we believe, is a comprehensive view of what one can expect while doing business in Mexico.

Mexico, as a country, is changing in all dimensions. It began its evolution from an almost totally agricultural economy after the Mexican Revolution of 1910. Recent presidents of Mexico have shown a strong probusiness bias and the result has been increased trade and industrial activity. The passage of the North American Free Trade Agreement (NAFTA) was as controversial in Mexico as it was in the United States. Nevertheless, NAFTA has increased business opportunities in Mexico.

We believe that the advantages of doing business in Mexico far outweigh the disadvantages. However, one must enter Mexico as a businessperson whose acumen is tuned to the Mexican frequency. Our hope is that this book will give the reader the ability to tune in to that frequency.

Finally, we want to thank our clients for the experiences that made this book possible. Perhaps most important, we wish to thank our wives for their patience while we completed this book.

Chapter 1

Introduction to Doing Business in Mexico

Foreign investment in Mexico is increasing. The consulting firm of A. T. Kearney has recently placed Mexico in the top ten countries in the world as attractive investment locales.[1] The passage of the North American Free Trade Agreement (NAFTA) helped to increase the attractiveness of direct investment and/or trade with Mexico.

However, doing business in any foreign jurisdiction poses a number of potentially serious legal and business risks. As trade with Mexico increases, the demand for information on potential risks and benefits of doing business in Mexico will increase. The purpose of this book is to provide information on the necessary, basic framework of legal and business concepts and practices upon which the Mexican business system is founded. One chapter is devoted to understanding the protocol and precepts of the social dynamics of interpersonal relationships, which are much more important in Mexico than in the United States.

This book is not intended to make the reader an expert, but rather to arm the reader with the basic knowledge that stimulates the right questions to ask. The book emphasizes establishing operations in Mexico as opposed to merely importing from Mexico or exporting to Mexico. That is, the book is about doing business *in* Mexico, not *with* Mexico, and the thrust is on exporting from Mexico.

WHY IS MEXICO ATTRACTIVE?

Before addressing how the book will accomplish its purpose, the reader will find it useful to understand *why* Mexico is such an attractive investment locale. Doing business in Mexico provides investors with several important competitive advantages.

These competitive advantages stem from the theory of "comparative advantage," a theory first advanced several hundred years ago that is the intellectual basis for free trade. Comparative advantage derives from an inherent or developed expertise or trade resource that allows specialization by a country in certain industries. For example, entrepreneurs attempting to grow mangoes in Finland will not use their resources to their best advantage. However, focusing those resources on fishing will be much more rewarding; mangoes can be imported.

Presumably, entrepreneurs in Finland will increase their standard of living more by taking advantage of the inherent resources at their disposal. Likewise, entrepreneurs of a land-locked tropical country can take advantage of the climate to grow mangoes, and their standard of living should increase more than if they began a fishing business. Therefore, both countries'entrepreneurs will be better off by using their respective comparative advantages.

Mexico, as a country, has several comparative advantages. These are discussed below.

Labor

The primary competitive advantage in Mexico is labor. Minimum wages in Mexico are set by law, by region, and by trade. The lowest minimum wage in the country is approximately equivalent to U.S. $3.00 *per day.* Although some regions, such as Mexico City and the northern border areas, have higher wages, the minimum often becomes the market rate. Appendix A details minimum wages by region and by trade.

Quality

The work product is quite competitive. Often, the stereotypical view of the Mexican workforce does not conform to reality. If the work product were not competitive in terms of quality, the number of exports to the United States and the number of firms moving plants to Mexico would not be increasing (see the next section).

Geography

Mexico is geographically close to the United States. This proximity significantly reduces transportation costs in comparison to transporting from Asia or South America, for example. Although the vast majority of *maquiladoras* are located on the northern border of Mexico, a growing number of companies are locating in other regions of Mexico.[2]

The Yucatán Peninsula, as an example, has become an important new region for foreign investors for several reasons related to its geography. The major port in the Yucatán, Progreso, is only 600 miles due south of New Orleans, as well as close to Miami, Tampa, and Houston. Essentially, along a 600-mile-wide border between Mexico and the United States, ocean freight is readily available to these U.S. ports from Progreso. Furthermore, companies considering exporting to the Caribbean and South America are well positioned geographically in the Yucatán, as the peninsula juts out into the Caribbean.

Relative Economic and Political Stability

Some readers may be surprised to read of the current relative stability, both economic and political, in Mexico. What follows can provide a perspective that is useful in understanding the current economic-political philosophy in Mexico compared to that of most Central and South American countries. Previously, this philosophy was centered around government restrictions on foreign investment, currency controls, and government ownership of many industries.

When Carlos Salinas, a Harvard-educated economist, was elected president in 1988, he began a program of privatizing industries that were previously government owned. He also worked to increase the confidence of foreign investors. As a result, the Mexican economy was strong until December 1994.

In December 1994, the new president, Ernesto Zedillo, was forced into a devaluation of the peso: it lost about half of its value against the dollar (from about three to about seven pesos to the dollar). The underlying causes were an artificially propped-up economy and political unrest in Chiapas, a state in Mexico. The combination of these factors created a loss of confidence in foreign investors, and the economy suffered as a consequence.

Mexico's economy bottomed out in 1995, and its gross domestic product (GDP) has steadily increased since that time. The inflation rate dropped from about 50 percent after the devaluation to an official rate of approximately 15 percent in 1999. Foreign investors began returning in 1995 and 1996. However, an informal devaluation occurred in late summer, 1998. The peso dropped on the open market from about eight to ten pesos to the dollar. Since that time, the peso has improved slightly against the dollar and the Mexican economy is slowly improving; the Mexican government repaid a bailout package ahead of schedule.

In the presidential elections of July 2000, Vicente Fox was victor. Mr. Fox was the candidate of the National Action Party (PAN), which ousted the ruling political party, the Independent Revolutionary Party (PRI), for the first time since the 1920s. The general sentiment is that Mexico now has a true two-party political system for the first time in over seventy years and that political stability will improve as a result.

NAFTA

NAFTA reduced many of the restrictions and barriers to trade between Mexico, the United States, and Canada and facilitated the leveraging of the comparative advantages that Mexico offers.

With respect to the textile and apparel industry, NAFTA further leveraged these benefits following the abolishment of the Multi-Fiber Agreement (MFA) in 1995. The MFA had established import quotas on textile and apparel products among the various signatories. After abolishing these quotas, the respective governments replaced the quotas with tariffs. However, under NAFTA the tariffs do not apply, further placing Mexico at a competitive advantage in the labor-intensive apparel-manufacturing industry due to the low cost of labor in this country.

Statistics Supporting Mexico's Attractiveness

The Center for the Study of Western Hemispheric Trade produced data indicating that U.S. imports from Mexico grew by about 160 percent from 1995 to 1998.[3] The *maquila* export industry in Mexico has grown at a phenomenal rate. According to the Mexican Department of Commerce (Secretaría de Comercio y Fomento Industrial [SECOFI]), the number of maquilas has grown from 1,920 in 1990 to over 2,600 in 1997. Furthermore, employment by maquilas[4] has increased by about 60 percent from 1990 to 1996.

Although maquilas are only one dimension of doing business in Mexico, these statistics provide empirical evidence that supports Mexico as an investment locale worthy of consideration. That is, something is occurring in Mexico's business environment that is causing companies to locate operations there. Our experience with Mexico has proved that investors are more than satisfied with their experience and return on investment. In fact, numerous investor companies are expanding their Mexican investments. All of these facts taken together are testimony to the potential that Mexico offers.

RISKS

An increasingly large number of companies are recognizing the economic benefits to locating in Mexico, but significant risks to operating in foreign jurisdictions do exist. The remainder of this book is devoted to educating the reader concerning the basics of operating a company in Mexico. The discussion includes the advantages, disadvantages, and associated risks and opportunities.

This purpose is accomplished by first discussing NAFTA and the maquila industry in Chapter 2. Abundant benefits can be obtained through NAFTA and the maquila industry, but companies must comply with copious requirements. Noncompliant companies could be in jeopardy of losing NAFTA benefits and/or face significant fines. A checklist of required licenses and permits is provided.

Transfer pricing is an issue that has created significant amounts of media coverage. The general concerns related to transfer pricing, the ability to receive "safe harbor" protection, and other issues are covered in Chapter 2 as well.

Chapter 3 discusses Mexican taxes, labor law, and the fiscal requirements of operating in Mexico. Mexican accounting and tax systems appear on the surface to be quite similar to U.S. systems. However, once the surface is scratched, numerous differences and subtle nuances appear that can create unpleasant consequences. Furthermore, the system is characterized by many "hidden costs" that a U.S. businessperson would not expect. Therefore, it is important to understand in advance the hidden costs and systematic differences to increase one's chance of success. Specific taxes and fiscal requirements are detailed for the reader.

A brief overview of U.S. tax implications related to doing business in Mexico is given in Chapter 4. These implications should be considered prior to beginning operations in Mexico. A basic understanding of the relevant aspects of U.S. tax law for foreign transactions can assist in planning the structure and organization of the foreign operation.

Chapter 4 also includes a discussion of the alternatives to and requirements for beginning an operation in Mexico. This discussion includes what types of Mexican entities are available and the general government requirements for initiating operations. The use of certain types of organizations can have important consequences for the availability of future alternatives.

The actual mechanics of importing and exporting may be well-known and understood by the reader. However, NAFTA requires some special documents be generated during the process, and these are discussed in Chapter 5.

Chapter 6 explains briefly the implications of foreign currency exposure that are inherent in multinational transactions. Improperly structuring transactions across borders or not protecting against possible currency exposure can potentially erase hard-earned profits.

The greatest nonbusiness issue facing those doing business in Mexico is not the language barrier; probably the majority of Mexican businesspeople with whom Americans will work speak English. The greatest issue concerns social protocol, which is much more important to doing business in Mexico than in the United States. Relationships, courtesy, and etiquette are critical to gaining the confidence of customers, suppliers, and employees in Mexico. Furthermore, the Mexican psyche is different from the American psyche, and this difference should be recognized before attempting to manage in Mexico. Chapter 7 discusses all of these differences and provides strategies for overcoming potential problems.

Chapter 8 provides an overview of tax implications related to U.S. citizens living abroad. Some ideas are presented to use in planning prior to moving.

Finally, the appendixes contain a list of minimum-wage rates by region, a Spanish-English financial glossary, an English-Spanish financial glossary, examples of Mexican financial statements, and useful government and business-related addresses in Mexico.

Chapter 2

Overview of the Maquila Industry and NAFTA

The potential benefits of doing business in Mexico have been leveraged even higher through public policy actions of both the American and Mexican governments that give special treatment to companies doing business under the maquila program and/or NAFTA. Although opinions to the contrary exist, the result is a net win-win situation for both countries, in our opinion. From Mexico's standpoint, public policy that attracts investment absorbs excess unemployment. Furthermore, Mexico benefits from the technology transfer that results when companies from developed countries locate plants within Mexico. Finally, foreign commerce generates foreign exchange for Mexico.

From the perspective of the United States, NAFTA has alleviated some of the competitive pressures from Asia and Europe due to relatively high U.S. labor rates. By locating in Mexico and transferring technology, U.S.-owned companies can take advantage of low labor rates. Furthermore, the geographic proximity of Mexico enables relatively low transportation costs in comparison to Asia or Europe.

In many respects, the maquila program set the stage for passage of NAFTA. Some believe that a separate maquiladora program and laws are obviated by the passage of NAFTA.[1] However, at this writing, the maquiladora program remains in effect.

THE MAQUILA PROGRAM

A maquiladora is a Mexican corporation (possibly a subsidiary of a U.S. company) that is allowed to import raw materials and equipment temporarily and duty free to Mexico for the purpose of assembling the raw materials into a component or final product. The maquila industry is sometimes referred to as an "in-bond industry," as any imported raw material and are under a bond or promise to be returned to the home country.[2]

The precursor to the maquila program was the *bracero* (day laborer) program begun in 1951. Under this program, Mexican farm workers could enter the United States on a daily or seasonal basis. The program was terminated in 1964 under pressure from U.S. farm unions.

The maquila program, begun in 1965, was initially restricted to a zone along the U.S.-Mexican border. Hence, maquilas were sometimes called "twin plants," as the U.S. parent company often owned a plant or facility on the U.S. side of the border and a Mexican subsidiary plant on the Mexican side.

Eventually, the maquila laws were changed to allow the establishment of maquilas within any part of Mexico. One factor driving the change was increased wage rates in the northern part of Mexico; unemployment was higher and wage rates were lower in other parts of the country. Minimum wage rates are set by region within the country. (See Appendix A for a recent schedule of wage rates by economic zone.)

One of the fastest developing areas of the country is the Yucatán Peninsula, which is composed of three states: Yucatán, Campeche and Quintana Roo. Although the Yucatán is relatively isolated, it has a number of significant advantages for foreign investment. First, it is geographically well situated, with regular ocean freight to the U.S. Gulf Coast, the Caribbean, and Central and South America. Labor rates in the Yucatán are the lowest in the country and workers are very loyal; low turnover rates are typical.

Maquiladoras receive certain privileges with regard to customs procedures, although most of these privileges are granted under NAFTA anyway. A special customs import document called a *pedimento* is required. Since raw materials are imported only for use in assembly, there are copious bookkeeping stipulations. All imports and subsequent exports through the maquila program must be accounted for and linked back to the pedimento; this is not a trivial bookkeeping matter. All in-bond imports must be exported or destroyed in Mexico. Noncompliance with the rules for tracking imported raw material can result in fines. For a more detailed discussion of the rules, see Chapter 5, Import/Export Requisites.

With the passage of NAFTA, maquilas have the right to sell within the domestic Mexican market a specified percentage of production output. This percentage increases with time and depends upon the specific product manufactured. However, the maquila must pay all applicable taxes on any products sold within Mexico, including tariffs, value-added taxes, and income taxes.

Requirements for Establishing a Maquila

The Mexican government has established certain prerequisites for a company to begin operations legally as a maquiladora. SECOFI, the Mexican equivalent of the U.S. Department of Commerce, must register the company in the maquila program and give permission to import and export. The following items must be presented to SECOFI:

1. Questionnaire: The purpose is to identify the types of materials imported, the product exported, and other relevant information that will become part of SECOFI's database.
2. RFC number: This is equivalent to the federal tax identification ID number (see Chapter 3).
3. Copy of the rental contract or deed to the property or factory that will be used: This may seem a strange request, but supposedly, one of the motivations behind this request is to determine if the company is involved in money laundering or drug trafficking. That is, it is assumed that the existence of a contract or deed lowers the probability that the company is involved in illicit conduct.

4. Mexican corporate charter: This charter is requested often in Mexico, for example, to open a business bank account. Presumably, the motivation is the same as with rental contracts and deeds.
5. Power of attorney for the person who will act as legal representative of the company in Mexico: Since the actual owners of the company are most likely foreigners and/or are not engaged in the daily operations of the business, this is required by SECOFI. Power of attorney is generally given to the general manager of the company.
6. Changes to the corporate charter: Any such changes must be filed.
7. Maquila contract: This contract specifies the terms of assembly between the U.S. company and the Mexican corporation. This requirement may seem an unusual demand, as contracts in the United States are generally confidential. The motivation is the same as in #3.
8. A favorable opinion from Secretaria de Desarrollo Urbano y Ecologia (SEDUE): SEDUE is the equivalent of the U.S. Environmental Protection Agency (EPA).
9. A complete list of machinery, equipment, and raw materials that are to be imported: This list must include description of the equipment, brand names, serial numbers, and value of equipment.

It is highly recommended that an attorney be retained to represent the company to SECOFI. A list of reputable attorneys can be obtained from the U.S. embassy or consulate in Mexico (see Appendix E for addresses).

Options for Doing Business in Mexico Through the Maquila Program

The maquila program provides three basic options for doing business in Mexico. Each has certain advantages and disadvantages. Each option is discussed here.

Contract Manufacturing

This is a low-risk approach to starting operations in Mexico. An existing Mexican company is contracted, usually on a per-piece basis, to assemble the product from raw materials temporarily imported from an American company. In the government's view they are temporarily imported because they *must* be exported either as a finished product or as a waste or as nontransformed raw material. The Mexican company assumes the responsibility for transportation and customs issues as well as manufacturing. The disadvantage to the American company is that the assembled product is usually more costly than if the American company owned the Mexican operation. Also, the American company maintains less control over quality and faces the risk of nonperformance.

Shelter Company

This is a variation of contract manufacturing, but the American company gains more control by placing high-level management and quality control personnel in the Mexcian operation. The Mexican company essentially provides local knowledge through middle-level management and physical facilities. These contracts usually are based on a cost per minute. That is, manufacturing companies often calculate the cost to operate a plant based on capacity defined as the number of workers multiplied by the number of minutes that can be worked over a specified period of time that corresponds to the costs to operate the plant. The resulting statistic is essentially the breakeven cost per minute of operation. The time in minutes to fabricate a particular product is estimated, or known based on previous experience. The cost per minute multiplied by the time in minutes to fabricate the product plus a profit factor is a traditional method to establish the contract price for these types of contracts. This is especially true of maquiladoras as the raw materials are temporarily imported and not purchased by the maquiladora.

A modification of the foregoing description is to import equipment temporarily from the American company to the Mexican shelter company. Sometimes the equipment needed is not readily available in Mexico.

Subsidiary of the American Company

In this option, the American company forms a subsidiary, usually manintaining 100 percent ownership.[3] The subsidiary then contracts with personnel and obtains all necessary permits to do business. The American parent normally provides management, at least at the upper levels. This approach reduces some of the attendant risks of the other two approaches but requires significant time for setup. Because local knowledge and contacts are very important, most American parent companies contract with attorneys and other consultants prior to beginning the paperwork.

Transfer Pricing and Safe Harbor

No businessperson or company should consider doing business in any foreign country without considering the potential risk of transfer price problems. Transfer prices are the amounts paid for the sale and purchase of goods between affiliated companies. The problem emanates from the possibility of evading taxes in one country or another. For instance, a parent company in the United States that buys a component or product from a subsidiary company in Mexico may have the ability to set the price in a way that reduces total taxes paid by creating artificial profit or loss between the two companies in different countries.

To illustrate the basic problem, assume that the U.S. corporate tax rate is 50 percent and the Mexican corporate rate is 25 percent. The parent will want to buy from the subsidiary at a high price in order to save taxes by creating low profits in the States and high profits in Mexico. For example, assume the Mexican subsidiary has a manufacturing cost of $5 for product X and the parent can sell product X in the United States for $20. The parent can set the purchase price at, say, $19 and report profits of $1 in the United States and $14 in Mexico. Total taxes are $4 ($14 × .25 [Mexico] plus $1 × .5 [United States]). On the other hand, if the parent pays less for the product, taxes will be higher, so that if the parent buys product X for $10 and sells it for $20, total taxes are $6.25.

The Mexican government will be happier with the results from the first example than with those from the second. The reverse is true for the U.S. government. Accordingly, both countries have rules governing the calculation of transfer prices.

Under Mexican law, the transfer price rules apply to all in-bond operations. That is, any company doing business as a maquila is potentially subject to the transfer price regulations even if the company is not a subsidiary of the parent. The burden is on the maquila to prove that the transfer price is reasonable given the circumstances. Most companies complied with this requirement in the past through one of two options: (1) transfer price study or (2) safe harbor.

The transfer price study is conducted by comparing similar companies in similar circumstances. Usually the study is conducted by an international accounting firm and is relatively costly. The safe harbor option is a Mexican regulation that allows the maquila to guarantee a tax payment using as a base for calculating the taxes the amount of approximately 7 percent of the assets used in the operation, including any assets temporarily imported to conduct operations or annual expenses, whichever is greater. After filing for this option, the maquila achieves safe harbor from any Mexican authority for transfer price problems.

Effective January 1, 2000, these regulations were amended to state that, in substance, if the maquila is controlled by some other entity, the controlling entity is considered the parent company, regardless of legal form. For example, if a U.S. company contracts with a nonaffiliated Mexican corporation, it is possible that the U.S. company could be considered the parent company of the Mexican corporation for purposes of transfer pricing rules if the definition of control is met. "Control" is defined in the regulations. The tax consequences could be adverse, as the U.S. company could fall under the definition of maintaining a "permanent establishment" in Mexico and would therefore be considered a Mexican taxpayer. Consequently, the U.S. company would be required to pay Mexican taxes under Mexican law. This could result in payment of taxes even if a loss was incurred under certain circumstances. Furthermore, this could subject the U.S. corporation to double taxation, as profits earned in Mexico may also be taxed in the States if the parent is deemed to have a permanent establishment in Mexico. (See Chapter 4 for more information.)

One strategy for overcoming the aforementioned adverse tax consequences for nonaffiliated companies is to structure operations so that the company purchasing the product does not legally control the maquila as defined in the transfer price regulations. There are many approaches to implementing this strategy, and a competent attorney and accountant should be consulted.

Fortunately, the new regulations continue to exempt a U.S. parent company from permanent establishment status if the Mexican subsidiary company files for safe harbor or conducts the aforementioned price study. In the event that the subsidiary does not comply with these regulations, there may be additional adverse tax consequences other than causing permanent establishment status.

Accounting

Any financial statements filed with the Mexican government must use Spanish and Mexican accounting principles. On the surface, Mexican accounting principles appear similar to U.S. generally accepted accounting principles (GAAP), with some significant differences. One is the required incorporation of the effects of inflation. A brief discussion of Mexican accounting principles is included in Appendix D, as well as examples of Mexican financial statements.

If the Mexican company is a subsidiary of an American company, consolidated financial statements are prepared in accordance with U.S. GAAP. Therefore, an accountant with knowledge of both Mexican and U.S. GAAP is necessary.

When Mexican financial statements are prepared and consolidated with those of an American parent, a currency translation gain or loss will occur due to currency differences: the Mexican subsidiary uses pesos and the American parent uses dollars. Because the peso value fluctuates against that of the dollar, currency translation gains or losses occur when pesos are converted to dollars. (See Chapter 6 for further discussion of this topic.)

The Future of the Maquila Program

At least two schools of thought exist concerning the future of the maquila program. One contends that the maquila program would no longer be needed once the second-phase NAFTA provisions kicked in on January 1, 2001. At that time, most maquilas would be able to sell 100 percent of their products in the Mexican market (there are some exceptions). Also, some favorable tariff treatment that maquilas received in the past was scheduled to be phased out in 2001.

Prior to NAFTA, all imports made by maquiladoras were not subject to import duties under the temporary import rules. Starting with the second phase of NAFTA in January 2001, any non-NAFTA component, raw material, or machinery imported, even if temporarily imported, is subject to import duties in Mexico. Although the import duties are subject to Most Favored Nation (MFN) rates, there is an incentive to source all goods with a NAFTA country.

Many believe, however, that NAFTA, coupled with remaining maquila laws, will make maquilas an even more competitive solution for U.S. and Canadian firms. Furthermore, many non-NAFTA companies with maquilas will lobby for continued maquila preferences. Regardless, low wages and free trade zone privileges will continue to be benefits for non-NAFTA countries.

Some believe that maquila growth will continue to be dramatic in medium- to small-size firms. This is because maquilas represent a low-cost way for the smaller firm to gain international exposure.

To date the second phase of NAFTA has not had much of an effect on the maquila program. However, in the year 2000 the United States signed a NAFTA-type agreement with the Caribbean basin countries. This treaty has had the effect of making some of these countries more competitive with Mexico and may have caused some U.S. contracts and investments to be diverted from Mexico.

In early 2000, Mexico signed a NAFTA-like agreement with several countries in Europe. At this writing, a NAFTA-type agreement is under negotiation between Mexico and several countries in both Central and South America.

OVERVIEW OF NAFTA

NAFTA is an international treaty signed by Mexico, the United States, and Canada. It is a comprehensive trade agreement that seeks to reduce restrictions and impediments to trade between the signatory countries in order to facilitate trade. The motivation for the treaty derives from the concept of comparative advantage discussed briefly in Chapter 1. It is almost as if the three countries are viewed as one economic entity with three separate currencies. The agreement itself numbers over one thousand pages.

The thrust of NAFTA is best understood by studying the objectives of the agreement:

1. Eliminate trade barriers and facilitate cross-border movement of goods and services
2. Promote fair competition in the free trade area
3. Increase investment opportunities in the free trade area
4. Provide protection and enforcement of intellectual property rights
5. Create procedures for implementation, application, administration, and resolution of disputes
6. Establish a framework for further cooperation and expansion of the benefits provided by the agreement

Clearly, NAFTA is designed to facilitate trade and investment between the signatory countries as well as to provide a framework for handling commerce and for resolving disputes.

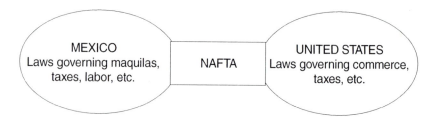

NAFTA essentially creates a conduit between the countries that provides economic and procedural advantages to companies that meet the NAFTA provisions. However, laws within each country and international laws remain in effect. Nevertheless, the laws within each country are changing to accommodate NAFTA provisions, which are outlined in the following material.

Tariffs and Nontariff Barriers

The agreement eliminates all tariffs over time. Although exceptions exist, in general, tariffs will be eliminated on a phase-out basis by 2003, ten years from the signing date. Furthermore, no signatory can impose new tariffs on another signatory.

The majority of import licenses are no longer required from a company with a national origin in a signatory country. This provision removes much of the uncertainty previously associated with obtaining licenses and significantly reduces costs and time associated with obtaining licenses.

Prior to NAFTA, a number of onerous requirements existed concerning local content of products, export performance, and other conditions that served to restrict trade. NAFTA eliminated these restrictions.

Rules of Origin

This is a critical provision because, to obtain NAFTA benefits, products must comply with the rules of origin. In general, the goods to be assembled or imported must have been made in North America.

Different rule of origin regulations affect each product and can become complicated to apply. The two basic rule types are tariff shift rule and value content rule.

Tariff Shift Rule

This rule allows the import/export of products between NAFTA countries using the beneficial NAFTA provisions even though some of the product content did not originate in North America. If a non-NAFTA raw material used in making the final product falls under a different tariff classification (using the Harmonized System of Tariff Classification),[4] then the final product will meet the rule of origin regulation. That is, the raw material must be deemed substantially transformed when incorporated into another product within the NAFTA country prior to import/export. For example, wood pulp (Chapter 47 of the Harmonized System) is imported to the United States for use in making paper (Chapter 48 of the Harmonized System).

Value Content Rule

This rule specifies a minimum value content of NAFTA origin for each product. Because there are different valuation methods, this can become complicated. For example, if fragrances are imported from South America to Mexico to be added to fragrances that are derived from Mexican sources, the final product could meet NAFTA provisions for export from Mexico depending upon the minimum value content required.

Cautionary Note

The foregoing describes only the general rules; numerous exceptions and product-specific requirements exist. The reader should research specific products of interest to determine their particular requirements and/or engage the help of a customs broker.

Customs Administration

NAFTA sets uniform rules, procedures, and forms for imported and exported goods that qualify for NAFTA treatment. This ensures greater predictability for all firms engaged in NAFTA commerce and reduces much of the previous uncertainty in dealing with customs offices.

A Uniform Certificate of Origin is required for any imported goods, and this certificate can cover multiple importations of that product for a one-year period. (See Chapter 5 for an example of a certificate of origin.)

Foreign Investment

In the past, Mexico had very restrictive foreign investment laws. One primary effect of NAFTA has been to liberalize foreign investment laws in Mexico. The investment provisions in NAFTA have also established a system for resolving disputes between foreign investors and NAFTA member governments. One objective of these provisions is to place foreign investors on an equal footing with domestic investors in a NAFTA country. As a result, NAFTA member governments are required to give equal treatment to foreign and domestic investors. To assist in this objective, foreign investors have the right to repatriate currency and the right to international arbitration in the event of disputes.

Investment is defined broadly in the agreement as a business (incorporated or not), securities, real property, or other property used in a business, and other types of investments such as loans and intangible property.

For many years, Mexico prohibited investment in certain "constitutional" industries that were controlled by the federal government of Mexico. However, a privatization initiative is under way that will ultimately open all industries to private investment.

Other Provisions

Numerous other NAFTA provisions are not discussed here. For example, many industry-specific rules and exceptions as well as additional provisions concerning such things as technical standards, services, intellectual property, antidumping, and so forth. The discussion of these items is beyond the scope of this chapter.

SUMMARY

The maquila regulations and NAFTA are the results of public policy actions by both the Mexican and U.S. governments to increase economic activity in both countries. These public policy actions are based on the respective comparative advantages of the United States and Mexico.

The maquila program allows temporary importations of raw material for the purpose of assembling the material into a product to be shipped back to the United States. No import or export duties are paid on either side of the border. Copious maquila regulations have been set by the Mexican government. Noncompliance with these regulations can result in fines that reduce the advantages of operating as a maquila.

Furthermore, both governments have transfer pricing rules and regulations that need to be considered. The purpose of these rules is to ensure that companies with operations on both sides of the border do not set prices on the product exported from Mexico in a way that unfairly reduces income taxes paid to either government.

NAFTA is a trilateral agreement between Mexico, Canada, and the United States. The purpose of the treaty is sixfold, but the major thrust deals with facilitating trade and investment among the three countries. Eventually, all tariffs and most other restrictions to trade among the countries will be eliminated, as if the three countries were essentially one economic entity, but with three separate currencies. To take advantage of the NAFTA provisions, companies must comply with the NAFTA regulations, which are numerous.

Although opinions to the contrary exist, we believe that NAFTA and the maquila program have had a net beneficial economic impact on the economies of the United States and Mexico. In our opinion, the future holds much promise for both countries to continue the positive impact on their respective economies.

Chapter 3

Overview of Mexican Taxes, Labor Law, and Fiscal Requirements

The accounting and tax systems in Mexico look quite similar to their counterpart systems employed in the United States. For example, the Mexican corporate income tax rate is 35 percent; Mexican financial statements more or less resemble those used in the United States. As a result, a superficial analysis could lead to the conclusion that the two systems are essentially equivalent. The consequences to this conclusion can be unpleasant.

An important pervasive difference in the two systems relates to culture. Taxpayers from the United States may consider the Mexican system to have an exaggerated emphasis on bureaucracy and paperwork. Also, numerous rules and regulations in the Mexican system focus on the *form* of filing and compliance.[1] Of course, it is not important whether one believes the U.S. system is more or less efficient; the Mexican system is the one that will be used.

The U.S. tax system is sometimes conceptually vague, which allows for interpretation and flexibility in terms of planning transactions. The Mexican system is less vague conceptually and more rigid, from the U.S. perspective, in terms of requirements to deem taxable deductions allowable. Any taxpayer found noncompliant with Mexican requirements is subject to significant fines. In fact, a system of fines built into the overall tax structure is an important revenue generator for the Mexican government.

A variety of taxes and legal requirements are imposed upon businesses. Discussed in this chapter are more than fifteen taxes and legally required labor benefits. In general, the additional burden in terms of payroll taxes and required benefits could increase overall labor costs by as much as 50 percent. Because labor costs are very low, the added costs may not be material in most projects. Nevertheless, the return on investment could be lower than what had been anticipated if these costs are not included in the original analysis. Furthermore, ignorance of these requirements is no defense for noncompliance. Noncompliance could cause the loss of the right to do business in Mexico.

There are additional hidden costs that may not be required by law, but by circumstance, that U.S. businesspeople might not anticipate. For example, sometimes companies find it necessary to provide meals, transportation, and other benefits to workers.

A proposed project cannot be properly evaluated without knowledge of the requirements discussed in this chapter. However, this chapter is meant merely as an *overview* of some very technical material. At the end, the reader should simply be aware of what questions to ask his or her technical advisor.

Before looking at specific taxes and legal requirements, there is one last consideration. The Mexican equivalent of the U.S. Internal Revenue Service (IRS) is Secretaría de Hacienda y Crédito Público (SHCP), commonly known as Hacienda. Hacienda divides all entities into either *personas morales* or *personas físicas.* Personas morales are the Mexican equivalent of corporations and personas físicas are individuals with taxable income. These distinctions are also important for banking accounts and in other situations.

INCOME AND OTHER NONPAYROLL
TAXES (FEDERAL)

Impuesto Sobre la Renta (ISR)

This translates literally as tax on rents. However, the definition of "rents" is different from what we in the United States would use. This is essentially the income tax, with a flat rate of 35 percent for both corporations and individuals.

For public policy reasons, the Mexican government has established provisions that allow reduced tax rates under certain conditions. If profits are reinvested, possibly taxes can be deferred so that the effective tax rate is reduced below 35 percent. Also, certain industries are given lower tax rates to assist them in development.

Income (or revenue) is defined basically the same as in the United States. That is, income represents sales from products or services. One important difference involves the effects of inflation on the computation of taxable income. Mexican law requires that taxpayers calculate the benefit that they receive from incurring debt during the time of inflation as a result of the decline in the purchasing power of the peso. For example, if a taxpayer had a debt of 100,000 pesos during the tax period and the official inflation rate was 10 percent, the taxpayer would have to report an income increase of 10,000 pesos as earnings from inflation effects.

The inflationary effect is also taken into consideration for assets, so that an inflationary loss, or deduction, can be taken. Therefore, depending on the company's net assets or liability position, the inflationary effect can have a positive or negative effect on net taxable income.

PRACTICAL TIP

Readers should avoid incurring debt in Mexico without compelling reasons to do so. If a U.S. parent transfers cash to a Mexican subsidiary that is expected to be more or less permanent, the transfer should most likely be considered equity. Recording the transfer as debt can trigger an increase in income due to inflation effects.

Operating expenses are also defined basically the same as in the United States. Again, however, there is an important distinction for qualifying expenditures as taxable deductions. To be deductible, an expenditure must be supported by a *factura* (see Figure 3.1). A factura is a special type of invoice. A note *(nota)* or receipt *(recibo)* is not the same as a factura. Notes or receipts will support taxable deductions under the U.S. system, but not under the Mexican one; a formal factura is required.

The depreciation provisions are very similar to those in the United States; a statutory percentage is allowed. Another option

FIGURE 3.1. Example of a Factura

ABC
S.A. de C.V
Calle 18 No. 108 x 23
Colonia Yucatan
97050, Merida, Yucatan
Tel: (99)20-0804
Fax: (99)20-4578
ganzoazu@prodigy.net.mx

Factura No: 50
Invoice No:

Consignatario: Consignee:	Address: Dirección:
Fecha: Date:	Condiciones de Pago: Payment Conditions:
Cliente: Client:	No. Pedido: Order No.:
Vía:	
Fecha de embarque: Shipping date:	Puerto de salida: Origin:
Destino final: Final destinant:	Términos de entrega: Delivery terms:

Orden No. Order No.	Descripción Description	Cantidad Quantity	Precio unitario Unit Cost	Total
			Subtotal	
			Fletes Freight	
			Impuestos Taxes	
			Total	

Cantidad con letra:

Notificar a:
Notify to:

Debo(emos) y pagaré (emos) incondicionalmente a la orden de O ABC   S.A. de C.V. Calle 18 No. 108 x 23 Colonia Yucatán 97050, Merida, Yucatán, México o en la misma plaza la cantidad de: Valor recibido a mi entera satisfacción. Si no fuera pagado a su vencimiento este pagaré causaría intereses moratorios a razón del   % mensual durante todo el tiempo que permanezca total o parcialmente insoluto sin que por ello se entienda prorrogado el plazo debiendo ser liquidado en la fecha de su vencimiento. De conformidad con el Art. 193 de la Ley General de Títulos y Operaciones de Crédito. Si el cheque es devuelto por fondos insuficientes se cobrará un 20% de indemnización.

Impreso: Enero del 2000 Folio del 01 al 50
Vence: Enero del 2002

_____
Nombre y firma de aceptación

allows for certain capital expenditures to become immediately deductible under certain circumstances, but only in specific regions of the country. Other provisions of the income tax law include loss carryforward and periodic tax payments.

PRACTICAL EXAMPLE

One maquila that subsequently became our client learned the distinction between facturas and recibos the hard way. After the first year of operations and the preparation of the annual tax return, the owner was surprised to learn that many of his expenditures were supported by recibos instead of facturas. The result—all expenditures not supported by facturas were denied.

Impuesto al Valor Agregado (IVA)

This translates as value-added tax but is actually a consumption, or sales, tax. It is generally referred to by its acronym, IVA, pronounced "eva." The rate is 15 percent normally, with a few exceptions. All facturas charge IVA, but notas or recibos do not. Therefore, it is possible to have transactions outside the tax system; that is, transactions evidenced by notes or receipts are not taxable, either from an income or an expense standpoint.

Expenditures lacking a factura to support them are classified as nondeductible expenses on the income statement. They are shown as a deduction from financial net income but are not allowed as taxable deductions. (See the final Practical Tip of this chapter for a possible method to convert these expenditures to deductible expenses.)

Any IVA paid is potentially refundable. To obtain the refund, a special tax form is filed with Hacienda. Mexican accounting software packages automatically record IVA paid during the accounting period in a separate receivable account.

It is important to note that IVA is not charged on exported products. For example, no IVA is charged on facturas that a maquila would issue for goods sold to a buyer in the United States.

Impuesto al Activo (IA)

This tax is translated as "tax on assets." The tax is calculated on net assets, or equity, and the rate is 1.8 percent. Under certain circumstances, this tax is not due. For example, if the ISR is greater than the calculated amount for IA, the IA is not payable.

Safe Harbor Tax

Recall the discussion in Chapter 2 concerning the safe harbor tax. Because maquiladoras are often owned or controlled by U.S. entities, a transfer price on the exported finished product can be set at a low amount to keep Mexican income taxes low. In order to guarantee that taxes are paid, maquiladoras may opt for the safe harbor tax in lieu of performing a transfer price study. This tax could be required if the Mexican corporation is a subsidiary of or controlled by a U.S. corporation. The amount of the tax is the greater of approximately 7 percent of assets or expenditures multiplied by the income tax rate. Total assets are calculated by combining the amount of the corporation's assets with any assets that have been temporarily imported.

Other Taxes

Impuesto Especial Sobre Producción y Servicios (IEPS)

This translates as "special tax on production and services." It is a tax on various types of commodities that are imported or produced. The rate varies depending on the commodity. The reader should investigate whether or not a particular product is covered.

Impuesto Sobre Automóviles Nuevos (ISA)

This translates as "tax on new automobiles." It is an excise tax on new cars, and the amount depends upon the value of the car.

Impuesto Sobre Tenencia o Uso de Vehiculos (ISTUV)

This is a use tax. It translates as "tax over the ownership or use of automobile." The amount of the tax depends upon the value of the car.

PRACTICAL TIP

A car titled and licensed in the United States may be temporarily imported without licensing the car in Mexico. However, the restrictions on use probably make this unfeasible for business purposes. For example, the foreign owner and his or her spouse are the only legal drivers of the car. If someone else is caught driving the car, the owner can be fined and the car confiscated. Furthermore, the car may not be used for commercial purposes under Mexican law.

Real Estate Taxes

When real estate is sold, taxes are collected at the closing. The tax collected is considered ISR. However, there are some special considerations for the sale of real estate. First, the basis, or cost, of the real estate is adjusted for various factors, including inflation. If, for example, the real estate was purchased for 100,000 pesos and the inflation rate has been 10 percent since the time of purchase, the adjusted cost for tax purposes becomes 110,000 pesos.

In Mexico, the legal purchase price is listed in a document called *escritura*. The escritura is the equivalent of a deed. An aqusition tax on the purchase is based on the purchase price. Although against the law, many purchasers ask that a lower price be placed in the escritura and that two checks be provided to the seller that equal the agreed-upon purchase price. That is, if the agreed-upon price is 300,000 pesos, the escritura might indicate the purchase price at, say, 200,000 pesos, and a separate check is then given for the additional 100,000 pesos. Buyers often agree to this because their taxes will be calculated on the lower amount recorded in the escritura.

Since this is fraud, many U.S. companies will not participate in this type of scheme. We advise the reader, especially as a foreigner, to stay strictly within the law, even though this may cost more in the short run. Recording the actual amount in the escritura is the correct thing to do legally and ethically. It also prevents problems in the future.

PRACTICAL EXAMPLE

One company with which we are familiar was in the process of acquiring a large tract of land when the seller demanded that the escritura record a lower sales price. The U.S. company balked at this suggestion. The Mexican seller demanded, for the sale to go through, that the U.S. company agree to pay an additional amount sufficient to cover the additional taxes the seller would have as a result of listing a higher amount in the escrituras. The U.S. company did just that.

PRACTICAL EXAMPLE

An acquaintance of ours purchased land in Mexico. Not being familiar with the law, he did not understand why he was asked for two separate checks at closing. He did not understand Spanish very well so he did not ask any questions.

He later decided to sell the land. He had paid a total of 800,000 pesos for the land but was chagrined to discover that the escritura recorded the purchase at 500,000 pesos. He ended up selling the land for 750,000 pesos, a loss of 50,000 pesos. However, since the escritura showed a cost of 500,000 pesos, he paid taxes on about 250,000 pesos of "profit" when he had actually sold the land at a loss.

The taxes previously discussed are federal taxes. Each state has its own set of taxes, and these taxes vary, although they tend to be minimal.

LABOR LAW AND TAXES

Unions in Mexico are quite strong politically, and workers have many rights and benefits beyond those normally received in the United States. Furthermore, it is difficult to terminate employees without incurring significant costs upon termination.

The paperwork required by the filing of payroll tax returns is more than U.S. businesspeople would expect. This adds to administrative costs. One possibility is to pay workers who are not entitled to benefits and for whom no payroll taxes are due. These workers are called *eventuales*. However, salaries paid to eventuales are not deductible for tax purposes. Deductible salaries for workers require the employer to pay payroll taxes. Workers receiving these salaries are called *asegurados*. Eventuales can become asegurados by law under certain conditions. There is a risk beyond the tax deductibility issue to the use of eventuales (see the following Practical Example).

PRACTICAL TIP

Some companies with a U.S. subsidiary may wish to pay eventuales' salaries, as they might be deductible by the U.S. subsidiary. This is not as straightforward as one might expect. Therefore, professional tax advice should be obtained before using this strategy.

PRACTICAL EXAMPLE

One client with whom we work did not have labor contracts with each employee despite our recommendation. Subsequently, a disgruntled employee who had been terminated went to a government office and claimed he had not received his proper severance pay as required by law.

The government will normally believe the worker without undisputable facts to the contrary. The worker claimed he had been employed for a number of years more than he actually had. Because there was no signed contract by the employee, the client was required to pay additional severance wages, even though his payroll records reflected actual employment dates.

The system is unfairly designed in favor of the workers. Once a worker files a complaint, the government office serves the legal representative of the company and sets a date for an informal hearing at the government office. The government representative hearing the complaint is, in theory, a neutral party. In practice, it is customary for the government representative to receive a "commission" from the worker based on the settlement received from the outcome of the hearing. Obviously, the government representative is predisposed to obtain as high a settlement as possible for the worker.

To represent the company at the hearing, we retained an attorney who held an important post in the same government agency.

(continued)

(continued)

(See Chapter 7—it is not uncommon for Mexican professionals to have more than one employer or to have "side" businesses.) Our presence at the hearing with an important attorney from the same agency had the effect of lowering the severance pay by more than half of the government representative's proposed settlement.

We highly recommend that each Mexican worker sign an employment contract with the company. Employers are legally required to put the terms of employment in writing by Articles 24, 25, and 26 of the Federal Labor Law. Actually, the contract can protect the company in the case of legal disputes with employees. The Mexican legal system strongly favors workers over employers. Therefore, contracts that cover the employment date and other specifics of employment can prevent future problems with disenchanted workers.

Employment contracts usually run for a relatively short period of time but can be renewed. Competent attorneys can provide a template from which to format the contract that includes the requisite clauses to protect the employer from false allegations.

Figure 3.2 is an example of an employment contract in Spanish. The reader is free to use it but should obtain professional advice as to its relevance to his or her particular situation.

FIGURE 3.2. Example of a Mexican Employment Contract

CONTRATO INDIVIDUAL DE TRABAJO

En la Ciudad de Mérida, Capital del Estado de Yucatán, a los siete días del mes de Junio de Dos Mil, los que suscriben el presente documento, por una parte la negociación, **S.A. DE C.V.,** en lo sucesivo **LA EMPRESA,** con domicilio en el predio marcado con el número ciento ocho de la calle dieciocho por veintitrés de la Colonia Yucatán de esta Ciudad, representada por la D.I. Claudia María Martínez Lusarreta y por otra parte la <u>Sra. María Isabel Gonzalez, en lo sucesivo **EL TRABAJADOR,**</u> con domicilio en el predio 142 de la calle X <u>entre 33 y 35 de la Colonia XXXXXXX</u> de esta misma Ciudad, hacemos constar: que hemos celebrado un Contrato Individual de Trabajo por 30 días, mismo que sujetamos al tenor de las siguientes:

(continued)

(continued)

CLAUSULAS

PRIMERA.—Los contratantes se reconocen expresamente la personalidad con la que se ostentan para todos los efectos legales a que hubiere lugar, y convienen que en el cuerpo de este Contrato contiene los términos y condiciones laborales conforme a los cuales se llevará a cabo la relación Obrero Patronal entre las partes, en términos de lo señalado en la Ley Federal del Trabajo.

SEGUNDA.—El trabajador manifiesta bajo protesta de decir verdad que tiene la capacidad y los conocimientos y aptitudes necesarias para prestar sus servicios personales como Costurera bajo la dirección, dependencia y subordinación del patrón, estando obligado a realizar también las actividades complementarias y trabajos generales afines a sus labores, debiendo desempeñar dichas actividades en el domicilio de la misma o donde el patrón ordene; para tal efecto el trabajador declara ser de nacionalidad MEXICANA de 32 años de edad, sexo Femenino, estado civil Casada.

TERCERA.—La duración del presente contrato será de 30 días y no podrá modificarse, rescindirse o terminarse sino en los términos y condiciones señaladas en la Ley Federal del Trabajo.

CUARTA.—Las partes acuerdan que la jornada de trabajo será matutina, de 48 horas, acumuladas, con horario de trabajo de Lunes a Viernes de las 8.00 a las 17.30 horas, con media hora de descanso a las trece horas y dos descansos adicionales de 10 minutos cada uno, estando obligado el trabajador a checar personalmente su tarjeta de asistencia o registrar su asistencia en los controles implantados por la Empresa.

QUINTA.—El trabajador contratado tendrá por cada cinco días de labores dos día de descanso que serán los sábados y domingos, con goce de salario íntegro, en mérito de la jornada acumulada.

SEXTA.—Las partes convienen que en los casos en que la Empresa requiera que el trabajador labore hora extra alguna o en sus días de descanso obligatorio, será indispensable una autorización por escrito del patrón al trabajador, señalándose claramente el horario y los motivos que generaron las horas extras o la jornada adicional.

SEPTIMA.—Las partes convienen en que el trabajador percibirá un salario diario de $ XXXX pagadero en el local de la Empresa los días viernes de cada semana, encontrándose incluido en éste, el pago correspondiente a los dos días de descanso; dicho salario será susceptible de los descuentos legalmente convenidos o autorizados por el trabajador.

OCTAVA.—Son días de descanso obligatorio los expresamente señalados por la Ley Federal del Trabajo.

NOVENA.—Los trabajadores que laboren más de un año de servicios en la Empresa disfrutarán de un periodo anual de vacaciones

(continued)

(continued)

pagadas por la Empresa, de seis días laborables y que aumentará en dos días laborables, hasta llegar a doce días; por cada año subsecuente de servicios; a partir del quinto año se aumentará dicho periodo en dos días por cada cinco años de servicios.

DECIMA.—Las partes acuerdan que la Empresa determinará el periodo de vacaciones que deberá disfrutar el trabajador, de acuerdo a las necesidades de la misma. El trabajador percibirá un 25 percent de prima vacacional sobre el salario que le corresponda durante el período de vacaciones.

DECIMA PRIMERA.—Los trabajadores que laboren un año de servicios en la Empresa disfrutarán de un pago en concepto aguinaldo de quince días, pago que será cubierto en los primeros veinte días del mes de diciembre de cada año.

DECIMA SEGUNDA.—Las partes declaran y aceptan que la violación a cualquiera de las obligaciones consignadas en este Contrato por parte del trabajador, será causa de rescisión del mismo sin responsabilidad para la Empresa.

DECIMA TERCERA.—Ambas partes declaran que conocen las obligaciones que la Ley Federal del Trabajo imponen a la Empresa y al Trabajador, en la inteligencia de que cualquier violación a la misma será causal de rescisión de Contrato con las consecuencias inherentes a dicha rescisión.

Leído que fue por ambas partes este Contrato ante los testigos que también lo firman y enterados todos de su contenido y sabedores de las obligaciones que contraen, lo suscriben por duplicado en la Ciudad y fecha señalados, quedando un ejemplar a cada una de las partes.

EL TRABAJADOR   LA EMPRESA

_____   _____
Sra. María Isabel Gonzalez   Lic. Juan Carlos Ramirez

Testigos

_____   _____
Sr. Luis Felipe Garcia   C.P. Sandra Maria Martinez

INDIVIDUAL EMPLOYMENT CONTRACT

In the city of Merida, capital of the state of Yucatan, on this seventh day of the month of June in the year two thousand, those who sign the present document are the following: on the part of the company, Anonymous Society of Variable Capital, herein referred to as THE EMPLOYER located in building number one hundred eight on

(continued)

(continued)

eighteenth street intersecting with twenty-third street in the neighborhood of Yucatan in this city of Merida, represented by Lic. Juan Carlos Ramirez; and by Ms. Maria Isabel Gonzalez, herein referred to as THE EMPLOYEE, residing in residence number XXX on street XXX between streets X and Y in neighborhood XXXXXXX in this city of Merida. Both parties declare that they have entered into an Individual Employment Contract for 30 days and are subject to the following:

CLAUSES

FIRST.—The parties expressly acknowledge the rights and responsibilities they individually possess for any and all legal matters which may arise and agree that this contract outlines the employment terms and conditions that shall be carried out in the employer-employee relationship in accordance with the Federal Employment Law.

SECOND.—The employee declares that s/he has the capacity, knowledge and aptitudes necessary to provide his/her personal services as <u>Dressmaker</u> under the direction, dependence, and subordination of the employer, being obligated also to carry out any additional activities and duties related to his/her position. The employee shall carry out these activities in the workplace of the employer or wherever the employer mandates. To such effect the employee declares the following: Nationality: <u>Mexican</u>; Age: <u>32</u>; Sex: <u>Female</u>; Marital Status: <u>Married</u>.

THIRD.—The duration of the present contract will be for 30 days and shall not be modified, rescinded, or ended unless under the conditions specified in the Federal Employment Law.

FOURTH.—The parties agree that the work week shall consist of 48 accumulated hours. The work week shall be from Monday through Friday from 8:00 to 17:30 with a thirty minute lunch period at one o'clock and two additional breaks of ten minutes each. The employee is obligated to check his/her time card or to register his/her attendance on the time clock installed by the employer.

FIFTH.—For every five working days, the employee shall have two non-working days which shall be Saturdays and Sunday. The employee shall receive the his/her integral salary for having worked the entire work week.

SIXTH.—The parties agree that should the employer require the employee to work overtime beyond his/her normal work day schedule or during his/her scheduled non-work days, it will be necessary for the employer to provide this request to the employee in writing. The employer shall clearly define the schedule and justification for the overtime hours or extended work week.

SEVENTH.—The parties agree that the employee shall earn a daily salary of $ XXXX payable in the place of employment each Friday. Included in this salary shall be the corresponding pay of the two non-

(continued)

(continued)

working days. Said salary shall be susceptible to any deductions legally acknowledged or authorized by the employee.

EIGHTH.—Those days expressly defined as non-working days by the Federal Employment Lay shall considered as such.

NINTH.—Those employees who have labored in said business for more than one year shall benefit from an annual vacation period paid by the employer. This vacation period shall be for six working days and shall increase in two-day increments for each subsequent year of service until reaching a maximum of twelve days. Starting from the fifth year of employment, said vacation period shall increase by two days for each five years of service.

TENTH.—The parties agree that the employer shall determine the vacation period from which the employee shall benefit, according to the needs of the employer. The employee shall receive a 25 percent vacation bonus in addition to his/her corresponding salary during said vacation period.

ELEVENTH.—Employees who labor in said business for one year shall benefit from a Christmas bonus equal to fifteen days of salary. This bonus shall be paid during the first twenty days of the month of December of each year.

TWELFTH.—The parties agree to and accept that the violation of any of the obligations outlined in this contract on the part of the employee will be cause for the cancellation of said contract without any responsibility on the part of the employer.

THIRTEENTH.—Both parties declare that they are familiar with the obligations that the Federal Employment Law imposes upon both the employer as well as the employee. The parties also acknowledge that any violation of these obligations will be cause for the cancellation of this contract as well as all consequences inherent in said cancellation.

Having read this contract in the presence of the witnesses named below, both parties acknowledge they understand its content as well as their obligations outlined herein and sign the present contract in duplicate in the city and on the date specified. A copy of the present contract shall be presented to both parties.

THE EMPLOYEE   THE EMPLOYER

_____   _____

Ms. María Isabel Gonzalez   Lic. Juan Carlos Ramirez

WITNESSES

_____   _____

Mr. Luis Felipe Garcia   C.P. Sandra Maria Martinez

A separate set of problems with labor involves health issues. Health problems among workers are much more common in Mexico. Normally, private health insurance is not provided to workers by the companies, although many do provide medical staff on premises. The Mexican social security system, *Instituto Mexicano del Seguro Social* (IMSS), does provide free health care to workers in IMSS health facilities.

When a worker misses work due to health-related issues, he or she should bring a document from IMSS proving that work was missed for health reasons. The worker is not paid for days missed.

PRACTICAL TIP

If a worker misses work and does not bring a signed form from IMSS, which is known as a permiso, the worker is sometimes penalized. The penalty takes the form of sending the worker home and not allowing him or her to work the day after missing work without a permiso. The worker will not be paid for the day missed as well as the day he or she attempted to return and was sent home.

The idea is to attempt to teach the importance of coming to work and the implications of disrupting the production process. In some cases, absence of this punishment would lead to an epidemic of missed workdays without permisos. This is because some Mexican workers are accustomed to living day-to-day, and if they are financially "ahead" for a day or two, they simply do not go to work because they "do not need the money." See Chapter 7 for additional discussion of this phenomenon.

PAYROLL TAXES

Participación de los Trabajadores (PTU)

This tax translates as "participation of the workers" and is the workers' share of profits. By law, the business is required to pay 10 percent of profits to workers. Nothing is paid if there are losses.

Instituto Mexicano del Seguro Social (IMSS)

This payroll tax, imposed by the Mexican Social Security Institute upon the employer, is approximately 17 percent of salaries paid. This rate varies significantly, depending on numerous factors for each employee. As in the United States, the amount subject to tax is limited to a base amount.

Sistema de Ahorro para el Retiro (SAR)

This translates as "savings system for retirement." This is over and above the PTU. The amount imposed upon the employer is 2 percent of salaries paid.

Instituto Nacional del Fondo de la Vivienda para las Trabajadores (INFONAVIT)

This translates as the "Fund for the National Institute of Housing for Workers." The purpose of this fund is to provide low-wage earners with low-cost mortgages for housing. The amount of the tax is 5 percent of salaries paid.

REQUIRED BENEFITS

Vacations

The amount of vacation time required per employee is based on years of service. The Mexican accounting system records this as a separate expense. Employees often accept this pay but do not take their allotted time for vacations.

Overtime

The government requires that overtime be paid at double the normal rate. The legal workweek is eight hours per day for six days. In actual practice, many companies work only five and one-half days, or forty-four hours. Some companies work the forty-four hours in a five-day span. However, companies are required to pay at least the minimum daily wage for seven days per week, even though the workweek may be only five days.

Legal Holidays

The government specifies seven paid legal holidays. In practice, many businesses observe an additional five to ten days of paid holidays for religious and state or national celebrations.

Aguinaldo

This is a required "Christmas bonus." The legal minimum is two weeks pay, but some companies pay more. The amounts may vary depending upon length of service.

Severance Pay

If an employee leaves of his or her own volition, a minimum of twelve days severance pay is required if the employee has fifteen or more years of service with the business. If an employee is terminated, the longer the service period, though, the greater the severance pay to which the worker is legally entitled. A statutory formula is used to calculate severance pay, but it is not always followed, even in government proceedings (see the Practical Example, p. 31).

Termination of employees "with just cause" is difficult. However, if accomplished, the employee is due at least three months severance. This can be true even if the company goes out of business.

The type of severance pay required when an employee is fired is called *liquidación*. When the employee resigns, the severance pay is called *finiquito*. Because the finiquito is less, employers generally attempt to convince the employee to resign rather than having to fire the worker. Regardless of whether the employee resigns or is fired, the employer should require the employee to sign a statement that he or she has received the full liquidación or finiquito and relinquishes future claims against the employer.

PRACTICAL EXAMPLE

A former employee of one of our clients became disgruntled and began to incite current employees. The employees began to quit and demand their finiquito. After receiving their severance pay, several of the employees went to the government claiming they were due additional severance pay.

The government served the employer with papers for an informal hearing. At the hearing, signed statements were provided proving that the former employees had been paid their due and that they had relinquished all future claims against the company. The case was dismissed.

OTHER BENEFITS

Numerous other benefits are quite normal. For example, many workers do not have cars or may not be able to afford public transportation, given their relatively low wages. As a result, it is not uncommon for a business to provide transportation by private bus from a pickup area to the plant.

Another benefit often provided is meals. Cafeterias are sometimes constructed in the plants, and meals are either partially subsidized or furnished free to workers.

An additional benefit sometimes provided is a *dispensa*. A dispensa is a basket of goods such as toliet paper and canned foods given to employees twice a month.

Sometimes medical facilities are also provided. These would include a full-time nurse or nurses and sometimes even an on-staff physician.

PRACTICAL EXAMPLE

One firm with which we have worked established a facility in a rather remote area of the country. In order to attract workers, the company bought and developed an area near the plant and built homes for the workers that were then sold to the employees at low prices and financed by the company. The company also built and operated a private school for the employees' children.

There is no question that the additional benefits provided will enhance loyalty. American companies may find some initial resentment going in, so any additional benefits that can be provided will most likely assist in overcoming potential problems.

FISCAL REQUIREMENTS

As mentioned earlier, the Mexican fiscal system is bureaucratic and paperwork oriented. Not complying with the details of the system may have adverse consequences. This section is meant to expand on some earlier comments about facturas and to give some of the details of the system. In subsequent chapters, especially Chapter 4, additional requirements for beginning operations and other issues are discussed.

A tax identification number is required by Hacienda. This is known as *Registro Federal de Contribuyentes* (RFC) (see Figure 3.3). After a company files for and receives the RFC, which is alphanumeric, Hacienda sends investigators to ensure that the address given is indeed where the business is domiciled. Companies face possible fines and penalties if there are differences between the application for the RFC and what the investigators discover.

Returning to the subject of facturas, there are numerous requirements concerning the printing of facturas. Facturas must be printed only in authorized printing shops, and must have printed on them the RFC stamp and be consecutively numbered by the printer. In addition, a factura is required to have imprinted on it the following information:

1. Name, address, and RFC number of the business issuing the factura
2. The name, address, and RFC number of the business or person to receive the factura (payor)
3. Quantity, type, and description of the product or service sold
4. The name of the printer and date of printing
5. Spaces for unit price, total price, and amount of IVA charged
6. Place and date of issue
7. Preprinted number of the factura

FIGURE 3.3. Example of an RFC Stamp

It is illegal not to issue facturas for all sales of products or services. The facturas document sales and deductible expenses by the purchaser of the goods or services to Hacienda. Without the proper specifications as described earlier, the facturas received will not support allowable deductions. Special provisions for facturas are issued by cash registers. However, facturas are to be issued only for valid revenues; they are not required when changing dollars to pesos.

PRACTICAL EXAMPLE

One company with which we became subsequently involved was advised to "facturize" transfers of dollars from the States to the Mexican company. These transfers were capital infusions. Nevertheless, because facturas were issued when the company exchanged the dollars to pesos, Hacienda treated the transfers as sales and the capital infusions were taxed as income, despite the owner's protests.

Often smaller enterprises are reluctant to issue facturas for services performed or products sold, thereby avoiding taxation. Other times you may be quoted a price with a factura or with a nota, the difference being that if no factura is involved, no IVA need be charged and the price will automatically be reduced by 15 percent. Therefore, facturas are not always received, meaning that no Mexican tax deduction will be allowed.

PRACTICAL TIP

If there is a U.S. parent of a Mexican company, one strategy for not losing deductions for the consolidated entity for nonfactura expenses is to have the U.S. entity sign an operating agreement with the Mexican entity to pay for the nonfactura expenses. There must be a valid quid pro quo involved.

For example, one company with which we are familiar owns a Mexican subsidiary. The two companies signed an operating agreement that provides for the U.S. company to conduct, free of charge, all marketing for the Mexican subsidiary. As a result, the U.S. company pays the nonfactura expenses of the Mexican subsidiary and deducts these expenses on the U.S. tax return, but it also receives a discount on purchases from the Mexican subsidiary.

We suggest hiring professional counsel before structuring an agreement.

SUMMARY

Mexican tax and labor laws are different from those in the United States in several ways. Knowledge of these differences prior to beginning operations in Mexico is important because operating without this knowledge can cause mistakes that only additional costs can correct. Furthermore, the Mexican tax, accounting, and government regulatory systems are designed in a manner that creates much more paperwork and management hierarchy than U.S. businesspeople normally encounter. The result is that analysis of projects without this knowledge will cause costs to be understated.

Various nonpayroll taxes are discussed in the chapter. Most of these taxes rely on the documentary evidence generated by facturas. All deductible expenditures must be supported by a factura, which is a formal invoice. Mere receipts for expenditures will not satisfy tax authorities, even if supported by paid checks.

The Mexican labor law and tax system is also quite different from the U.S. system. Numerous payroll taxes and various legally required employee benefits are imposed on employers. Furthermore, due to cultural differences and for economic reasons, it is normal for larger companies to provide additional benefits, such as transportation, meals, and so forth. Therefore, one should be careful in using minimum wage rates alone for analysis purposes. We generally add an additional 40 percent to labor rates to estimate total labor cost with benefits.

Due to the very important differences between the U.S. and Mexican systems, we highly recommend employing the services of a competent consultant to advise on how to approach a specific project. The major U.S. accounting firms all have offices in Mexico, and numerous competent Mexican firms have English-speaking personnel who can assist you. Contact the U.S. embassy or a U.S. consulate for assistance in locating consultants (see Appendix E).

Chapter 4

Beginning Operations in Mexico: Basic Considerations, Alternatives, and Requirements

There is no substitute for planning. A well-thought-out plan can make the difference between disaster and success. Planning becomes even more crucial if one considers the potential problems that can increase exponentially when the economic entitites involved are operating in more than one country. The various alternatives for structuring the entity or entities involved and the different methods of arranging transactions may each have different business and tax implications.

The purpose of this chapter is to introduce the reader to basic considerations, alternatives, and government requirements of starting a business in Mexico. These ideas can be incorporated into the plan of initiation.

This chapter is divided into two parts. First, tax and business considerations from the U.S. side are discussed, since a U.S. citizen or corporation is likely to be involved. The second part of the chapter is designed to educate the reader about available alternatives and government requirements to begin operations in Mexico.

U.S. TAX AND BUSINESS CONSIDERATIONS

Chapter 2 discussed beneficial NAFTA provisions and tariff breaks afforded maquilas. Although NAFTA and the maquila program are definite advantages to operating in Mexico, a broader focus for analysis should be used that includes the tax and general business consequences to creating a multinational entity. Normally, entities are present in both countries. That is, a U.S. citizen or corporation controls an entity in Mexico. Tax and legal entities can take various forms in both countries, but whatever forms are chosen, the entities involved must comply with tax requirements in two countries.

Both Mexico and the United States have established governmental policy to accommodate intercountry trade and investment. NAFTA is an example of this. Another example is a tax treaty signed by the governments of both countries. The treaty is briefly summarized in the next section as the beginning point for a discussion of taxes.

U.S.-Mexico Tax Treaty

As the title indicates, one of the primary objectives of the treaty is to avoid double taxation, that is, to avoid taxing of the same income by both governments. This is accomplished by laying out concepts of allocation of income and expense between the two tax jurisdictions, Mexico and the United States. The other prime objective is to prevent the evasion of taxes. The purpose of this section is to familiarize the reader with the big picture.

An important starting point is to know whether the Mexican entity meets the definition of a "permanent establishment," which is defined in Article 5 of the treaty. The definition covers almost any type of operation that has an address in Mexico. If the company meets the definition of a permanent establishment, it is required to pay taxes in the host country (Article 6). If the company merely transacts business through an independent agent, broker or contractor, it is not considered to be a permanent establishment.

Legally established maquilas were exempted from the permanent establishment definition in the past. However, as of January 1, 2000, the law changed and a maquila is now considered a permanent establishment of the U.S. parent. This could have some serious adverse consequences, which are discussed in the next section, Business and Tax Planning.

Regardless of which country taxes the income, Article 24 of the treaty gives relief from double taxation (in most cases). Since both countries tax worldwide income, relief from double taxation is accomplished by each country allowing a tax credit for income taxes due in the home country that were paid to taxing authorities in the other country. The specific rules affecting the tax credit are set within each country; the treaty merely established the conceptual agreement between the two countries.

In most cases double taxation can be avoided. Nevertheless, it is possible for additional taxes to be imposed. For example, one of the business entity forms that may be adopted in Mexico is a "branch." A branch is simply an appendage of the parent company; it is not a separate legal entity. Although there are advantages to adopting the branch form as a method to conduct foreign operations, one of the disadvantages is that it could trigger an additional tax of 5 to 10 percent (Article 11A). This is known as a "branch tax."

Finally, Article 27 of the treaty provides for exchange of information between the two countries. The purpose of this article is to inhibit the abuse of tax and other laws in either country to evade legally owed taxes in either jurisdiction. Note that *evasion* of taxes is illegal, whereas *avoidance* of taxes can be accomplished legally.

Business and Tax Planning

The virtues of business and tax planning are well known and well understood. The mistake that is sometimes made is to make decisions without the necessary facts. Because each case is likely to be significantly different, the objective of this section is to present basic information from which to make informed decisions, or at least to provoke proper questions of business and tax counsel.

However, one imperative that is not case-specific should be heeded if your Mexican company is a maquila: avoid having your Mexican company meet the definition of a permanent establishment. If a U.S. company is deemed to have a permanent establishment in Mexico, the result may be double taxation, despite the tax treaty's objective of avoiding double taxation. The permanent establishment will pay Mexican taxes for which the U.S. company may not be entitled to a U.S. tax credit. This is because under U.S. tax law the income of the permanent establishment that is a maquila may not be considered foreign source income for the U.S. company. Since the United States taxes worldwide income, the U.S. company will pay taxes again in the States.

The basic U.S. tax objective with respect to foreign taxes is to enable U.S. companies to compete in foreign countries and avoid double taxation. As previously mentioned, this objective is accomplished through tax credits. However, these tax credits are subject to numerous limitations. Furthermore, such credits are available only for income taxes. Mexico has a number of taxes that are not income taxes (see Chapter 3). Also, U.S. tax credits are available only for taxes paid in another country on what is defined in the United States as foreign source income. As stated earlier, maquilas that are considered permanent establishments do not generate foreign source income.

Another important decision to make prior to beginning operations involves the choice of the entity through which to do business in Mexico. Assuming a U.S. corporation is involved, the choices are branch, subsidiary, joint venture, or hybrid entity. Each choice has its own tax implications.

Branch

A branch is a facility of the U.S. corporation and is not considered a separate legal entity. It most likely will be considered a permanent establishment and will be required to pay Mexican taxes. However, the income of the branch should qualify as foreign source income under U.S. tax regulations, and, therefore, a U.S. tax credit is allowable for Mexican income taxes paid. Recall that the branch may be required to pay a branch tax. An advantage to this form is that if the branch operates at a loss, the loss can be used to offset income earned by the U.S. parent.

Subsidiary

A subsidiary is a legally incorporated entity that is separate from the U.S. parent. (See the next section on the possible corporate forms available in Mexico.) A subsidiary will most likely be considered a permanent establishment and would pay Mexican income taxes. U.S. tax laws would consider the subsidiary's income as foreign source income, but it is not taxable until distributed to the U.S. parent. (Recall that if the subsidiary is a registered maquiladora and complies with certain conditions, the parent company is not considered to have a permanent establishment.) Therefore, a subsidiary may offer the potential to plan the use of tax credits by controlling when the income is distributed. Another advantage to a subsidiary is that Mexican governments (local and state) may offer tax holidays and/or incentives, but only to legally incorporated Mexican corporations, which a subsidiary would be.

Since a subsidiary is a separate legal entity, it may insulate the parent from legal liability, whereas a branch would not. A subsidiary may also be beneficial from an image standpoint. That is, the subsidiary will have a name that identifies it as a Mexican company, even though it may be owned by an American corporation.

Joint Venture

A joint venture in its purest form is simply an arrangement between two entities to operate a business. The joint venture can take various legal forms. For example, a joint venture can be legally established as a separate corporation or by two corporations or other entities signing a contract to operate a business. If two corporations establish another corporation, it is simply a partially owned subsidiary of two parent companies. The tax implications of the joint venture depend upon the types of entities that compose the joint venture.

Joint ventures are an especially viable option for American companies doing business in Mexico. Mexican business practices and laws are quite different. For this reason, many companies have chosen to do business under the joint-venture structure, using a Mexican national or Mexican company as a partner in the venture. This approach lowers the risks to the U.S. company by increasing knowledge of local customs, laws, and business practices.

PRACTICAL EXAMPLE

Vulcan Materials is a Fortune 500 company that has done business in many foreign jurisdictions. Vulcan decided to commit several hundred million dollars to a mining project in Mexico. At the time, Mexican law required a Mexican partner. The law has since changed, but Vulcan claims that the law would have no effect on their decision if they were to do it again.

The CEO of the joint venture (also CEO of a Vulcan subsidiary) stated, "The fact is that there are important differences in the way business is conducted in Mexico, and our [Mexican] partners have proven themselves extremely skilled in those areas." (*Source:* Profile: A publication of Vulcan Materials, Vol. 14, 1992. "Up and Running in Mexico," Tom Ransdell, p. 6.)

Hybrid Entities

Beginning in 1997, U.S. tax rules were liberalized to provide potential tax benefits to corporations, partnerships, or individuals with foreign operations. Under certain circumstances, a hybrid entity can be created that allows the U.S. tax entity to be treated as a partnership in the United States and as a corporation in the foreign country. A reverse hybrid entity is treated as a corporation for U.S. tax purposes and as a partnership in the foreign country. The implications are potentially beneficial from tax planning perspectives, allowing deferral of income or loss under certain circumstances. Tax counsel should be sought to determine if this is a worthwhile consideration given the reader's particular situation.

Transfer Pricing Note

Regardless of the entity form adopted, if there are transactions between the foreign entity and the U.S. entity, transfer pricing is likely to be an issue (see Chapter 2 for a further discussion of transfer pricing). Remember that if either government determines that transfer prices were set in a manner to avoid taxes in one country or the other, significant penalties may be assessed.

There are numerous accepted methods for setting transfer prices and an array of variables to be considered. Explanation of the transfer price-setting methods is beyond the scope of this book; a qualified accounting firm should be consulted. The end result should be a transfer price that is based on market conditions and/or an arm's-length transaction.

STARTING OPERATIONS

The best advice about starting a business in Mexico that we can give is the most obvious—obtain a competent attorney. An attorney will accomplish most of what follows in this section. However, the reader will know his or her objectives better than the Mexican attorney, and discussion in the following pages is meant to assist the reader in knowing his or her options and understanding better the attorney's advice.

Structuring Operations in Mexico

The previous section covered the alternatives from the U.S. perspective. Since a Mexican entity will be involved, the alternatives in Mexico must be considered as well. The decisions to be made are, of course, case specific, and decisions made in one country may have tax or legal implications for the other country. For these reasons, the following discussion summarizes the various Mexican legal entities.

Corporation

The Mexican equivalent of a corporation has three options. The name for a corporation is *sociedad,* but the same term is applied to partnerships. The three types of corporations are discussed here.

Sociedad anónima (SA) (anonymous corporation). The legal minimum of capital required to form an SA is 50,000 pesos, and the number of shareholders is unlimited, but the minimum number of shareholders is two. The legal *maximum* amount of capital is fixed by the corporate charter.[1] The amount of fixed capital may be subsequently changed, but only through a change in the corporate charter. Amendment of the corporate charter is a relatively involved process. For this reason, most Mexican corporations adopt another form, *sociedad anónima de capital variable* (SA de CV) (anonymous corporation with variable capital).

SA de CV types of corporations have corporate charters that allow for the legal capital to vary without amendment of the corporate charter. This provides much greater flexibility in selling more shares. The number of shareholders is unlimited. The minimum amount of legal capital is the same, 50,000 pesos.

As in the United States, both the SA and the SA de CV forms provide for limited liability of stockholders *(accionistas)*. Nevertheless, board members may become personally liable for misdeeds of the corporation.

Sociedad de responsabilidad limitada (SRL) (limited responsibility corporation). This is similar to a closed corporation in the United States. It has a lower legal minimum for capital, 3,000 pesos. The number of shareholders is limited to fifty. The SRL has both the variable and fixed capital options and fewer legal requirements such as the requirement for an auditor.

Partnerships

As in the States, Mexico has two basic forms of partnerships: general and limited liability. *Sociedad en nombre colectivo* is the equivalent of the general partnership; *sociedad en comandita* is the limited liability partnership equivalent.

Joint Venture

Technically a pure joint venture can be formed through a joint venture contract that creates a separate entity for the sole purpose of operating the joint venture. This entity is called *asociación en participación* (AP). Our experience has been that when two corporations decide to form a joint venture, it is done through the creation of a separate corporate entity, as opposed to the AP form.

Sociedad Civil (SC)

The SC is essentially a general partnership used by professionals such as lawyers and accountants. The number of partners is not limited. Each partner has unlimited personal liability, as in all general partnerships.

Branch

A branch is identified as *sucursal de sociedad extranjera* (S de SE), which translates literally as "branch of a foreign corporation." As discussed previously, this type can pose an image problem for the foreign parent company, and certainly the foreign parent's assets will be legally at risk for all activities of the branch.

Also, the branch must register with SECOFI and report to other government agencies. It may also have to pay a branch tax in Mexico. For these reasons, most U.S. companies establish a subsidiary as a Mexican corporation.

Agents

Another method to begin operations in Mexico is through agents. There are advantages to using agents, some of which have already been discussed.

An agent could be a broker, a representative, a distributor, a contract manufacturer, and so forth. One of the principal advantages to using an agent is that the U.S. company will most likely avoid creating a permanent establishment in Mexico. A principal disadvantage is that the U.S. company loses a great deal of control over the process that the agent is undertaking.

If the decision is made to use an agent of some kind, the reader should be very careful to determine whether a permanent establishment has been created. In most situations, this will probably not be the case. However, if an inventory is maintained in Mexico but owned by the U.S. company, the Mexican subsidiary is likely to be considered a permanent establishment. At a minimum, this arrangement will require a Mexican tax return. Of course, take precautions to get all details worked out ahead of time and in writing. Although putting agreements in writing is always a good idea, it is especially so in Mexico. Even then, be careful not to become too

---

PRACTICAL EXAMPLE

We have a client who opted to obtain an independent agent to perform certain services within Mexico for the client. Soon the independent contractor began to make demands that changed the nature of the agreement. Of course, the changes were to the independent contractor's benefit and to the detriment of the client. The contractor had become aware of the acute dependence on him by the client.

When the client resisted the changes on the basis of the signed contract, the contractor agreed that he had signed the contract but responded ominously that "things have changed now." There had been no change in work or market conditions, but the contractor had sensed a reliance on him and was confident that the client had no alternative but to accept the new terms.

To maintain the continuity of the operation, we advised the client to accede to the demands of the contractor but to delay their implementation. A search for a replacement was immediately begun. Astonishingly, the replacement soon began to make demands to change the nature of the arrangement. We advised hiring another agent who could share the work to defeat the impression that the client was unduly reliant on one contractor.

---

reliant and dependent upon one individual or company. Certainly have a "plan B" ready to implement if "plan A" fails.

The tendency of many Mexicans is to view events always in the most opportunistic sense. The result is a predisposition to focus on the short run and to take advantage of a current situation at the expense of a long-term relationship that could prove very beneficial. Chapter 7 discusses in more detail the proclivities for this type of philosophy.

Legal Requirements to Begin Operations in Mexico

If the decision is made to incorporate, a company faces more legal requirements than if operations are begun as a branch. Nevertheless, branches must file with Hacienda, SECOFI, and the Secretary of Foreign Relations. If the operations to be established fall under maquila rules, see Chapter 2 as well.

Assuming a Mexican corporation is to be formed, the reader will of course need an attorney. Two general types of civil attorneys are found in Mexico. For important documents, be sure to see an attorney who is a *notario publico,* which is an attorney who has the right to file and register documents that are to become a part of what Americans would call the public record, as well as enforceable legal documents.

Just as in the States, the attorney will first obtain permission from the government for the use of the corporate name that has been chosen. Depending on various circumstances, this approval may take a week or more.

Next the attorney will prepare the *acta constitutiva,* which is the corporate charter and by-laws. If you do not speak Spanish, an interpreter will be named for you in the charter. In general, the basic provisions are what would be expected in the United States, with some differences. First, a Mexican corporation will have to specify the duration of the corporation, which can be changed in the future. Also, the charter will identify the capital as being fixed or variable, as discussed ealier. The charter will specify the type of management, either *administrador único* or *consejo de administración,* which are discussed later. The charter will identify an auditor *(comisario),* who has somewhat different objectives than the independent auditor in the States.

In addition, non-Mexican nationals who are stockholders must sign an agreement stating that they agree to be bound by Mexican law and will not seek diplomatic protection in case they or the corporation run afoul of the law. Non-Mexican stockholders must have a valid visa to sign the acta constitutiva (see later explanation of visas).

After incorporating, but before starting operations, other applications, filings, and permits must be obtained. The first requirement is to obtain an RFC number from Hacienda (see Chapter 3). Most government applications and permits will ask for this number, as it is the equivalent of the U.S. federal ID number and is required to show the entity as registered with the Hacienda.

To ensure limited liability of the stockholders, the company should register with Registro Público de la Propiedad y del Comercio, which formally advises the public that the company is doing business as a corporation. Otherwise, it is possible that the stockholders could be held liable personally for corporate actions.

If foreign stockholders are involved, the corporation must file with Registro Nacional de Inversiones Extranjeras (Foreign Investment Registry) and also with a branch of SECOFI, Dirección de Inversion Extranjera (Office of Foreign Investment). The SECOFI filing is annual.

If the corporation will import any materials, it must file an application with a department of Hacienda called Padron de Importadores (Register of Importers). Also, recall that maquilas, which involve temporary imports, must file with SECOFI under the requirements for the maquila program (refer to Chapter 2).

Prior to contracting with employees, the company must register with the following government agencies:

- IMSS (social security)
- INFONAVIT (national housing fund)
- SAR (federal pension fund)

Remember also that contracts are required by law for all employees (see Chapter 3).

The company is also legally required to register with Instituto Nacional de Estadística Geografía e Informática (INEGI). This government agency collects statistics on many variables.

In years past, corporations were required by law to join one of several different quasi-government agencies that are similar to chambers of commerce for specific industries. The rules have been liberalized, but corporations must join Sistema de Información Empresarial Mexicano (SIEM), the Mexican business information system.

Prior to beginning manufacturing operations, a registration must be made with Secretaría de Medio Ambiente, Recursos Naturales y Pesca (Semarnap), a government agency similar to the U.S. EPA. Some types of operations will also require permits from the Secretary of Health.

In most locales in Mexico, commercial zoning is not required. However, it is necessary to obtain what is known as uso del suelo, which is a land use permit. This is issued by the local authorities and relates to specific use.

A non-Mexican may not work legally in Mexico without a proper visa. Work visas are known as FM-3 or FM-2, nonresident and resident visas, respectively.

The time required to complete these legal requirements could vary considerably. The most optimistic estimate is probably a month, but plan on three months. All of the foregoing requisites are summarized in a checklist at the end of this chapter.

Considerations in Locating Your Place of Business

Mexico is a large and culturally diverse country. Depending upon the area of the country in which a company will locate, the reader may be faced with different types of considerations. If a plant is to be located in a major industrialized area, such as the northern border of Mexico, Monterrey, or Mexico City, the considerations are similar to those in the United States. For this reason, the discussion here focuses on the lesser-developed regions of Mexico.

As discussed in Chapter 1, the wage rates in the more developed areas of Mexico have increased. Although there are definite advantages to locating in the more developed areas, the primary economic advantage to locating in Mexico is low wages, and that advantage is significantly eroded in the more developed areas. It is for this reason that new foreign investment is targeting undeveloped areas.

However, the unique conditions in the less-developed regions require special attention by the investor prior to buying or renting a location. First, the potential investor will most likely not have much personal knowledge concerning market conditions, for example, price, location, and so forth. The same is often true in the States, but there the potential investor has ready access to a more or less reliably established market through real estate agents, chambers of commerce, and so on. Furthermore, prices are established based on market conditions; little consideration is given to one's ability to pay.

The distinctions in Mexico can be dramatic. Fortunately, each Mexican state has an economic development office with a knowledgeable, English-speaking staff. However, the Mexican business community is often closed and tightly networked. The result is that the reader could receive a narrow view of the facts through government offices; that is, the staff may be accustomed to dealing only within the tight circle of friends and relatives, and other available options may never be provided. Also, if the potential investor is perceived as a wealthy American or American company, that investor may face inflated prices.

To further aggravate this problem, the market may not be very well developed. Mexican real estate agents and brokers do not have multiple listing services, so there is generally no way to get a good picture of the market by consulting one source. Real estate advertisements in the classified section of the paper usually do not give prices and asking prices are generally much higher than the "real" prices that would be accepted. Obtaining an accurate picture of the market may take considerable time, unless the reader is able to locate a trustworthy source.

PRACTICAL EXAMPLE

One client came to Mexico in search of land through the economic development office of the state. Free land in a village near the capital had been offered to the client. An appointment was set with the mayor of the village. The mayor never showed for the appointment, leaving the client stranded for several hours.

The client subsequently traveled with the state representative to interview the owners of an industrial park that was privately owned. Although the park was quite modern, the prices offered were higher than stateside equivalents.

Finding this unsuitable, the client asked the state representative for help in finding a location. The state representative obligingly took the client to a relative in the real estate business. The relative was wealthy and not very interested in investigating the market. All locations shown were completely unacceptable to the client. At this point, the client was ready to abandon the project as impractical.

We explained the situation to the client and how the game was played. That is, the state representative was working within a small group of friends and the real estate market was not well established. We suggested that the client give us three weeks to locate a suitable site at an appropriate price. After an intensive study, within two weeks several alternatives were presented, and the client is now manufacturing clothes very successfully.

Considerations Involving Employees

The United States has a very mobile society. This is not quite the case in some regions of Mexico. Although most mid- and upper-level management employees will have their own transportation, most other employees will not. Nevertheless, Mexico has a well-developed network of public transportation—buses.

Lower-level employees cannot afford cars or taxis. Therefore, the bus routes and transportation network must be taken into account when choosing a factory location. Some companies augment employee salaries by a nominal amount to assist with payment of bus fares, which usually are from two to four pesos one way.

If employees cannot arrive at work easily through the public transportation system, the company may have to provide private transportation such as a company bus. This bus would collect employees at a designated place and time. This is an added capital expenditure, involving the cost of the bus as well as operating costs for a driver and fuel. Fuel is expensive in Mexico; at the time of this writing, a gallon of gasoline costs just over the equivalent of U.S. $2.50, which is about 60 percent higher than the current U.S. price.

Forethought must be given to availability of workers, especially in remote areas. Other factories may already exist in or near the area chosen by the reader. If so, the preexisting factory may already employ the available workforce. In such a case, the two companies will end up in a bidding war for employees.

Consideration must also be given to eating arrangements. Many companies build cafeterias within their plants and subsidize the cafeteria programs.

PRACTICAL TIP

One way to partially offset the cost of a cafeteria is to provide meals as part of an incentive plan. For example, if a worker produces at least 110 percent of his or her quota for the previous week, the worker will receive free meals. This also serves as an open example for other workers of the benefits of productivity.

If the chosen site is in a very remote area, other costs will most likely be incurred. For example, one company with which we have worked developed a quarry in a very remote section of Mexico. To attract the number of workers needed to operate the quarry, the company had to build homes for employees as well as operate a private school for the workers' children.

Infrastructure

We take many things for granted in the States that may not be readily available in Mexico. For example, adequate water supply with sufficient pressure is needed for some types of fabrication. Transportation infrastructure such as railroads, highways, ports, and airport facilities should be investigated.

Assuming infrastructure needs are met, a potential investor should consider more detailed and technical problems that could arise. For example, a company moving into an existing plant may discover that the plant is equipped with one-phase electricity. Since most modern electric machinery requires three phases to operate efficiently, this problem must be corrected and will have a cost.

In the States, this is a simple fix. In Mexico, it may not be. One of the obstacles to doing business in Mexico is the amount of government paperwork required. Because government bureaucrats responsible for issuing licenses and permits do not make much money and because bribery (mordida) (tips, if you prefer) is a long-standing tradition in Mexico, companies should be prepared to include provisions for this in their budgets.

PRACTICAL EXAMPLE

We assisted one U.S. client with starting a sewing factory from the ground up. After locating an appropriate existing factory, a lease and contract for remodeling was negotiated. The client had to install a transformer and substation at his own expense; the electric company, which is federal, does not provide this equipment. However,

(continued)

(continued)

the equipment and the installation must be approved by the Comisión Federal de Electricidad (Federal Electric Commission).

Final approval in this case took three months. The bureaucrat at the commission had wanted a bribe and the contractor had not paid it. We indicated to the contractor that we had contracted for the installation, and if a bribe was required, that was his responsibility. We did make a call to a friend at the commission; eventually the installation was completed, probably through the combination of a bribe and our call.

This example provides insight into negotiation in Mexico; everyone plays hardball. The bureaucrat and the contractor knew the plant had to be up and running or the client would lose production. Even though the contract included a deadline for completion, we made sure the client always owed significant amounts to the contractor. Be sure to take the proper position from the beginning, or the cost of doing business will increase.

The aspects of doing business in Mexico discussed here could be construed as disadvantages. However, in our opinion, if a potential investor analyzes a prospective investment in Mexico as a "package," the advantages will far outweigh the disadvantages. Nevertheless, the potential investor should analyze from a standpoint of complete information.

Other Considerations

Other considerations and likely questions of which an investor should be aware are discussed in this section.

100 Percent Ownership

Mexican law now allows 100 percent foreign ownership of Mexican corporations; that is, the law does not require a Mexican citizen as a stockholder or even director. However, a foreign stockholder must have a Mexican tax identification number (RFC).

Legal Representation

The Mexican legal system requires that all corporations have a representante legal (legal representative). This is a much more substantive position than that of the registered agent of corporations in the United States. The representante legal must sign all contracts and government documents. This individual must be extremely trustworthy because he or she can borrow money, file lawsuits, and essentially is the human embodiment of the corporation.

The representante legal may be a foreigner or a Mexican citizen. Many companies name the general managers of their plants as their legal representatives. Whoever is named, the representante legal should reside in the country and be available in case of unexpected litigation or needed execution of a contract. If unexpected litigation is filed against the company, and its legal representative is unavailable, the company will go unrepresented at judicial proceedings and may lose by default, regardless of the merits of the case. Some types of legal proceedings require almost immediate presence of the representante legal to defend charges; the Mexican system is sometimes not as slow as in the United States.

PRACTICAL TIP

To avoid the potential problem of no legal representation, a limited power of attorney can be given to someone to act as the representante legal in specific circumstances, e.g., defense against lawsuits (but not for the filing of lawsuits). Also, a limited power of attorney can be given to someone, such as the controller, to file and sign certain government documents that are routinely required. This removes from the representante legal some of the burden of being constantly present.

Consejo de Administración or Administrador Único

Recall that one of the choices in forming a corporation is to designate the policy-setting arm of the corporation as consejo de administración or administrador único. The former is the equivalent of a board of directors, and the latter (single administrator) is essentially a board of directors of one. In either case, the person or persons may or may not be stockholders.

Comisario

Mexican law requires that all corporations have the equivalent of an auditor, called comisario responsable para inspección y vigilancia (commissioner responsible for inspection and vigilance). This requirement is irrespective of the size of the corporation, number of shareholders, whether the company's stock is traded on the Mexican stock exchange, or any other factor.

The comisario cannot be an employee or relative of a board member. However, the comisario may be a stockholder. Numerous duties of the comisario are outlined in the law, but this person is not required to be a *contador público* (CP) (Mexican equivalent of a CPA).

Ownership of Real Property

Mexican law has been liberalized to the extent that, in most cases, foreigners may own real property in Mexico. A notable exception is if the property is within the so-called "prohibited zone," which is within fifty kilometers of borders or beaches. Nevertheless, a Mexican corporation with foreign ownership may own real property in the prohibited zone if the reason is to use the property for productive purposes.

Another approach to owning land in the prohibited zone is to acquire land through the use of a *fidecomiso,* which is a trust operated by a bank. The property is owned by the trust, and the trust is required to follow the foreign investor's instructions. The bank will of course charge a fee. The authors know of no cases involving legal problems with ownership through a fidecomiso.

Regardless of how the real estate is acquired, foreign investors need to be aware of the tradition of acquiring real estate at false prices. The tax and legal systems in Mexico enable fraud in the acquisition of real estate. It works as follows: A legal document that is the equivalent of a deed (escritura) is prepared. This document specifies the legal purchase price, which is the basis for calculating taxes due upon closing of the sale. The amount stated in the escritura may or may not be the actual amount paid for the property, but it is the amount used for legal and tax purposes. Important implications of this system need to be considered prior to the purchase of real estate. (Refer to Chapter 3 for additional information on taxes and the sale of real estate.)

Vehicles

Cars and trucks may be imported temporarily to Mexico. However, they may not be used for commercial purposes. Furthermore, only the owner and his or her spouse may legally drive the vehicle. Therefore, all vehicles used for business purposes should be acquired in Mexico and have legal Mexican license plates.

SUMMARY

This chapter illustrated that a significant amount of planning is a prudent and important step prior to beginning operations. The planning process should include consideration of taxes in both countries.

Appropriate consideration should be given to the unique aspects of operating a business in Mexico. Without foreknowledge of what considerations are important, serious mistakes could be made that doom the enterprise to failure. Many of the considerations described here could be viewed as disadvantageous relative to what would be encountered in the States. Nevertheless, if the entire project is viewed as a complete package, the net advantages should outweigh the disadvantages. Mexico has had many more success stories than disasters, and investors are still arriving.

Checklist for Beginning Operations in Mexico

- Choice of business entity
- If corporate form chosen
  - obtain approval of name
  - file corporate charter *(acta constitutiva)*
  - decide on administrador único or consejo de administración
  - appoint representante legal, and
  - obtain a comisario (auditor)

- Obtain federal ID number (RFC)
- Register with Registro Público de Comercio
- Register with Registro Nacional de Inversiones Extranjeras
- Comply with various requirements
  —Hacienda
  —SECOFI
  —Secretary of Foreign Relations
- Before contracting with employees, register with
  —IMSS (social security)
  —INFONAVIT (national housing fund)
  —SAR (federal pension fund)
  —Hacienda of the state
- Obtain labor contracts for each employee
- Register with INEGI
- Join SIEM
- Register with Semarnap
- Ensure that you have the proper uso del suelo
- Obtain a business permit issued by the city
- Obtain proper visas

Checklist for Locating a Plant

- Consider the existing transportation network
- Obtain data to determine availability of workers
- Make eating arrangements
- Ensure that appropriate infrastructure is available

Chapter 5

Import and Export Requisites: A Summary

Certain import and export procedures are uniform worldwide. However, there are specific requisites to import into or export from Mexico when NAFTA and/or maquila rules apply. Therefore, the purpose of this chapter is to provide a basic summary of import and export requirements under NAFTA or maquila regulations.

NAFTA REQUIREMENTS

As previously discussed, the critical requirement to obtain NAFTA treatment is to prove origin of the product or component that is imported. This is done formally through completing a certificate of origin.

The certificate of origin has explanations for what is to be entered into each space on the document. A blank certificate of origin is shown at the end of this chapter (see Figure 5.1). The exporter must include the harmonized system (HS) tariff classification of the product or products exported (see field 6 on the form). A listing and description of all HS codes can be accessed at <www.census. gov/foreign-trade/schedules/b/index.html>.[1]

Note that field 7 (preference criterion) is the key to proving that the goods may receive preferential NAFTA treatment (please refer to Chapter 2 for a more in-depth discussion of the rules of origin). Recall that if the goods exported are not wholly obtained or produced in one of the three countries, they may still qualify for NAFTA treatment. Additional information can be obtained through requesting documents number 5001 through number 5005 from the U.S. Department of Commerce. It may be advisable to seek professional counsel before making the final determination.

The NAFTA treaty provides for verification of origin by the importing country's customs officials. This is done principally through questionnaires and/or telephone interviews. Customs officials may also make verification visits. Customs officials of the importing country conduct these visits in the exporting country. Written notification of a planned visit is required.

Any exporter filing a false certificate of origin is subject to penalties. If concerns exist about whether a product will qualify for NAFTA treatment, confidential advance rulings can be obtained.

If it is determined that the product does not meet NAFTA origin requirements, there is still the possibility of somewhat favorable tariff treatment through the "most favored nation" tariff rate. A customs broker should be consulted for assistance.

For the importer to receive preferential tariff treatment under NAFTA, the exporter must complete and sign the certificate of origin, either in English, Spanish, or French, at the exporter's discretion. However, customs officials of the importing country may request a translation. The certificate of origin remains in effect for a twelve-month period for additional imports of the same goods, as listed in the certificate of origin.

Because goods imported under NAFTA receive favorable tariff treatment and due to the ease with which a certificate of origin can be forged, customs agents from all three countries closely scrutinize these forms.[2] Apparently, as a result of this crackdown, customs agents are realizing that many exporters do not understand how to complete the forms. As a result of these problems and the complexities of the documentation, some shipping companies are beginning to offer NAFTA documentation as a part of their service to customers.

TEMPORARY IMPORTS UNDER
THE MAQUILA PROGRAM

Chapter 2 discussed the requirements for enrollment in the maquila program. Before any product can be imported under the auspices of this program, the maquila must have received from SECOFI a letter titled "Maquila Program Approval and Assignment of Registration Code" (Aprobación de Programa de Maquila de Exportación y Asignoción de Clave de Registro). After receiving the registration code, SECOFI will provide another letter that authorizes an import under the registration code that has been assigned. The letter will authorize the import of only certain categories of items. Each type of product that is authorized to be imported duty free as a temporary import is listed under one of two classifications in the authorization letter: (1) raw material, parts, components, and packing material or (2) machinery, tools, equipment, and equipment parts. Products in the first category may remain in the country for up to eighteen months; those in the second category for up to five years, and this can be extended.

Nothing will be allowed into Mexico that is not listed in the authorization letter. Future additional authorization can be requested if the maquila will be importing materials or equipment not listed in the original authorization letter.

Before an import occurs, the maquila must send copies of the aforementioned letters from SECOFI to the customs broker. The maquila should request an advance copy from the exporter of all products being sent. The list should contain, as a minimum, the following:

- Number of items
- Serial number of each item
- Item description
- Unit price

Maquila management should then translate the list to Spanish and enter the information onto a special "invoice," indicating it is a temporary import under the maquila program. This invoice is then sent to the customs broker.

When the goods arrive, the customs broker will conduct a preinspection. Every item in the container is checked against the description and serial number in the list on the special invoice. Any discrepancies can be corrected on the special invoice that will be shown to customs. It is important that this preinspection be done, as Mexican customs authorities review these import documents very carefully against actual shipments. Any discrepancies noted by customs can cause delays in getting the goods through customs and/or fines.

PRACTICAL EXAMPLE

We are familiar with a case involving a U.S. company with a maquila in Mexico that sent two containers in one shipment to Mexico. The bill of lading incorrectly listed one pallet in container 1 as included in container 2. Customs officials would not allow either container to pass through customs until a relatively large fine was paid.

In this case, had the Mexican customs broker conducted a preinspection, the mistake could have been found and corrected, and the delay and fine could have been avoided.

The maquila's customs broker will provide a document called a pedimento, which is numbered.[3] The pedimento is a special document that indicates when, where, and how the imported items entered the country, and that these items are imported on a temporary basis. The pedimento contains a complete list of items that were included on the special temporary import invoice.

The pedimento is a critical document. Mexican law requires that all merchandise entering the country as a temporary import be strictly accounted for and controlled. All raw material or components imported under the maquila program must be exported in the form of an assembled product. Any excess raw material must be exported back to the original exporter or destroyed under the supervision of Mexican customs.

The reason for such strict control is because the raw material entered the country duty free for the express purpose of being assembled and exported. Until NAFTA provisions have been 100 percent phased in, maquilas would have an unfair advantage if allowed to import duty free and sell in the Mexican market. Therefore, customs maintains tight control over the disposition of items temporarily imported.

The pedimento becomes the key to accounting for each item. Mexican customs can audit the maquila to ensure that the law is followed and that all temporary imports are properly accounted for by the maquila. The maquila is required under law to set up a database to track items imported, quantity used, quantity remaining, and a staggering array of other data. The pedimento is the document that enables the development of an audit trail. Fortunately, various computer programs are available to assist with the record keeping.

Due to the new maquila regulations effective beginning 2001, it is especially critical to maintain impeccable records of temporary imports. As discussed in Chapter 2, any imports that are from non-NAFTA countries are now subject to duty even if temporarily imported. Failure to strictly comply with the copious regulations on record keeping associated with temporary imports can cause the imposition of significant fines.

Mexican customs utilizes a random selection method to determine which imports will be selected for customs revision. Customs will review the data in the pedimento against the actual goods received. As stated earlier, the actual goods received must conform to the data in the pedimento to the slightest detail in order to avoid delays and penalties. Therefore, the initial preinspection by the customs broker is quite important and can identify problems and correct them prior to reaching Mexican customs.

SUBSEQUENT EXPORT OF ITEMS TEMPORARILY IMPORTED

As previously discussed, all items temporarily imported must ultimately be accounted for by a company (the maquila). The maquila is responsible for maintaining records that can tie raw materials imported to assembled products exported.

REPORTS REQUIRED TO BE FILED
WITH THE MEXICAN GOVERNMENT

Over forty reports may be required to be filed under Mexican customs law concerning imports, exports, and movement of imported goods and equipment. Not all of these reports apply to each company; nevertheless, normally a significant number of them do. Therefore, most companies involved in export/import have at least one staff member that devotes his or her time to complying with the government's requirements.

SUMMARY

Various special import/export requisites exist under NAFTA and maquila rules. Customs officials on both sides of the border are scrutinizing the paperwork carefully. Therefore, it is important to pay close attention to the details.

Under NAFTA rules, the key document is the certificate of origin. This document establishes the ability to obtain preferential NAFTA treatment. A customs broker or shipping agent can be of great benefit in completing the form properly.

The pedimento is the critical document for temporary imports under the maquila program. The regulations require that all imported material be linked to the pedimento and tracked through this document while in the country.

FIGURE 5.1. NAFTA Certificate of Origin

DEPARTMENT OF THE TREASURY
UNITED STATES CUSTOMS SERVICE

Approved through 12/31/96
OMB No 1515-0204
See back of form for Paper-
work Reduction Act Notice

NORTH AMERICAN FREE TRADE AGREEMENT
CERTIFICATE OF ORIGIN

Please print or type
19 CFR 181.11, 181.22

1. EXPORTER NAME AND ADDRESS	2. BLANKET PERIOD (DD/MM/YY)
	FROM
	TO
TAX IDENTIFICATION NUMBER:	
3. PRODUCER NAME AND ADDRESS	4. IMPORTER NAME AND ADDRESS
TAX IDENTIFICATION NUMBER:	TAX IDENTIFICATION NUMBER:

5. DESCRIPTION OF GOOD(S)	6. HS TARIFF CLASSIFICATION NUMBER	7. PREFERENCE CRITERION	8. PRODUCER	9. NET COST	10. COUNTRY OF ORIGIN

I CERTIFY THAT:

• THE INFORMATION ON THIS DOCUMENT IS TRUE AND ACCURATE AND I ASSUME THE RESPONSIBILITY FOR PROVING SUCH REP-
RESENTATIONS. I UNDERSTAND THAT I AM LIABLE FOR ANY FALSE STATEMENTS OR MATERIAL OMISSIONS MADE ON OR IN CON-
NECTION WITH THIS DOCUMENT;

• I AGREE TO MAINTAIN, AND PRESENT UPON REQUEST, DOCUMENTATION NECESSARY TO SUPPORT THIS CERTIFICATE, AND TO
INFORM, IN WRITING, ALL PERSONS TO WHOM THE CERTIFICATE WAS GIVEN OF ANY CHANGES THAT COULD AFFECT THE ACCU-
RACY OR VALIDITY OF THIS CERTIFICATE;

• THE GOODS ORIGINATED IN THE TERRITORY OF ONE OR MORE OF THE PARTIES, AND COMPLY WITH THE ORIGIN REQUIREMENTS
SPECIFIED FOR THOSE GOODS IN THE NORTH AMERICAN FREE TRADE AGREEMENT, AND UNLESS SPECIFICALLY EXEMPTED IN
ARTICLE 411 OR ANNEX 401, THERE HAS BEEN NO FURTHER PRODUCTION OR ANY OTHER OPERATION OUTSIDE THE TERRITORIES
OF THE PARTIES; AND

• THIS CERTIFICATE CONSISTS OF [   ] PAGES, INCLUDING ALL ATTACHMENTS.

11a. AUTHORIZED SIGNATURE	11b. COMPANY
11c. NAME (Print or Type)	11d. TITLE
11e. DATE (DD/MM/YY)	11f. TELEPHONE NUMBER (Voice) (Facsimile)

Customs Form 434 (121793)

FIGURE 5.1 *(continued)*

DEPARTMENT OF THE TREASURY
UNITED STATES CUSTOMS SERVICE

Approved through 12/31/96
OMB No. 1515-0204 See
Customs Form 434 for Paper-
work Reduction Act Notice

NORTH AMERICAN FREE TRADE AGREEMENT
CERTIFICATE OF ORIGIN CONTINUATION SHEET

19 CFR 181.11, 181.22

5. DESCRIPTION OF GOOD(S)	6. HS TARIFF CLASSIFICATION NUMBER	7. PREFERENCE CRITERION	8. PRODUCER	9. NET COST	10. COUNTRY OF ORIGIN

Customs Form 434A (121793)

NORTH AMERICAN FREE TRADE AGREEMENT CERTIFICATE OF ORIGIN INSTRUCTIONS

For purposes of obtaining preferential tariff treatment, this document must be completed legibly and in full by the exporter and be in the possession of the importer at the time the declaration is made. This document may also be completed voluntarily by the producer for use by the exporter. Please print or type:

FIELD 1: State the full legal name, address (including country) and legal tax identification number of the exporter. Legal taxation number is in Canada, employer number or importer/exporter number assigned by Revenue Canada; in Mexico, federal taxpayer's registry number (RFC); and in the United States, employer's identification number or Social Security Number.

FIELD 2: Complete field if the Certificate covers multiple shipments of identical goods as described in Field # 5 that are imported into a NAFTA country for a specified period of up to one year (the blanket period). "FROM" is the date upon which the Certificate becomes applicable to the good covered by the blanket Certificate (it may be prior to the date of signing this Certificate). "TO" is the date upon which the blanket period expires. The importation of a good for which preferential treatment is claimed based on this Certificate must occur between these dates.

FIELD 3: State the full legal name, address (including country) and legal tax identification number, as defined in Field #1, of the producer. If more than one producer's good is included on the Certificate, attach a list of additional producers, including the legal name, address (including country) and legal tax identification number, cross-referenced to the good described in Field #5. If you wish this information to be confidential, it is acceptable to state "Available to Customs upon request". If the producer and the exporter are the same, complete field with "SAME". If the producer is unknown, it is acceptable to state "UNKNOWN".

FIELD 4: State the full legal name, address (including country) and legal tax identification number, as defined in Field #1, of the importer. If the importer is not known, state "UNKNOWN"; if multiple importers, state "VARIOUS".

FIELD 5: Provide a full description of each good. The description should be sufficient to relate it to the invoice description and to the Harmonized System (H.S.) description of the good. If the Certificate covers a single shipment of a good, include the invoice number as shown on the commercial invoice. If not known, indicate another unique reference number, such as the shipping order number.

FIELD 6: For each good described in Field #5, identify the H.S. tariff classification to six digits. If the good is subject to a specific rule of origin in Annex 401 that requires eight digits, identify to eight digits, using the H.S. tariff classification of the country into whose territory the good is imported.

FIELD 7: For each good described in Field #5, state which criterion (A through F) is applicable. The rules of origin are contained in Chapter Four and Annex 401. Additional rules are described in Annex 703.2 (certain agricultural goods), Annex 300-B, Appendix 6 (certain textile goods) and Annex 308.1 (certain automatic data processing goods and their parts). NOTE: In order to be entitled to preferential tariff treatment, each good must meet at least one of the criteria below.

Preference Criteria

A The good is "wholly obtained or produced entirely" in the territory of one or more of the NAFTA countries as referenced in Article 415. Note: The purchase of a good in the territory does not necessarily render it "wholly obtained or produced". If the good is an agricultural good, see also criterion F and Annex 703.2. *(Reference: Article 401(a) and 415)*

B The good is produced entirely in the territory of one or more of the NAFTA countries and satisfies the specific rule of origin, set out in Annex 401, that applies to its tariff classification. The rule may include a tariff classification change, regional value-content requirement, or a combination thereof. The good must also satisfy all other applicable requirements of Chapter Four. If the good is an agricultural good, see also criterion F and Annex 703.2. *(Reference: Article 401(b))*

C The good is produced entirely in the territory of one or more of the NAFTA countries exclusively from originating materials. Under this criterion, one or more of the materials may not fall within the definition of "wholly produced or obtained", as set out in Article 415. All materials used in the production of the good must qualify as "originating" by meeting the rules of Article 401(a) through (d). If the good is an agricultural good, see also criterion F and Annex 703.2. *(Reference: Article 401(c))*

D Goods are produced in the territory of one or more of the NAFTA countries but do not meet the applicable rule of origin, set out in Annex 401, because certain non-originating materials do not undergo the required change in tariff classification. The goods do nonetheless meet the regional value-content requirement specified in Article 401 (d). This criterion is limited to the following two circumstances:

   1 The good was imported into a NAFTA country in an unassembled or disassembled form but was classified as an assembled good, pursuant to H.S. General Rule of Interpretation 2(a), or

   2 The good incorporated one or more non-originating materials, provided for as parts under the H.S., which could not undergo a change in tariff classification because the heading provided for both the good and its parts and was not further subdivided into subheadings, or the subheading provided for both the good and its parts and was not further subdivided.
NOTE: This criterion does not apply to Chapters 61 through 63 of the H.S. *(Reference: Article 401(d))*

E Certain automatic data processing goods and their parts, specified in Annex 308.1, that do not originate in the territory are considered originating upon importation into the territory of a NAFTA country from the territory of another NAFTA country when the most favored nation tariff rate of the good conforms to the rate established in Annex 308.1 and is common to all NAFTA countries. *(Reference: Annex 308.1)*

F The good is an originating agricultural good under preference criterion A, B, or C above and is not subject to a quantitative restriction in the importing NAFTA country because it is a "qualifying good" as defined in Annex 703.2, Section A or B (please specify). A good listed in Appendix 703.2B is also exempt from quantitative restrictions and is eligible for NAFTA preferential tariff treatment if it meets the definition of "qualifying good" in Section A of Annex 703.2. NOTE 1: This criterion does not apply to goods that wholly originate in Canada or the United States and are imported into either country. NOTE 2: A tariff rate quota is not a quantitative restriction.

FIELD 8: For each good described in Field #5, state "YES" if you are the producer of the good. If you are not the producer of the good, state "NO" followed by (1), (2), or (3), depending on whether this certificate was based upon: (1) your knowledge of whether the good qualifies as an originating good; (2) your reliance on the producer's written representation (other than a Certificate of Origin) that the good qualifies as an originating good; or (3) a completed and signed Certificate for the good, voluntarily provided to the exporter by the producer.

FIELD 9: For each good described in field #5, where the good is subject to a regional value content (RVC) requirement, indicate "NC" if the RVC is calculated according to the net cost method; otherwise, indicate "NO". If the RVC is calculated over a period of time, further identify the beginning and ending dates (DD/MM/YY) of that period. *(Reference: Articles 402.1, 402.5)*

FIELD 10: Identify the name of the country ("MX" or "US" for agricultural and textile goods exported to Canada; "US" or "CA" for all goods exported to Mexico; or "CA" or "MX" for all goods exported to the United States) to which the preferential rate of customs duty applies, as set out in Annex 302.2, in accordance with the Marking Rules or in each party's schedule of tariff elimination.

For all other originating goods exported to Canada, indicate appropriately "MX" or "US" if the goods originate in that NAFTA country, within the meaning of the NAFTA Rules of Origin Regulations, and any subsequent processing in the other NAFTA country does not increase the transaction value of the goods by more than seven percent, otherwise "JNT" for joint production. *(Reference: Annex 302.2)*

FIELD 11: This field must be completed, signed, and dated by the exporter. When the Certificate is completed by the producer for use by the exporter, it must be completed, signed, and dated by the producer. The date must be the date the Certificate was completed and signed.

Customs Form 434 (121793)(Back)

Chapter 6

Foreign Currency Risk:
A Primer

All companies are subject to normal business risks such as lack of demand for products, strikes by workers, and so forth. When operating internationally, new dimensions are added to the risks encountered. Previous chapters discussed various risks associated with doing business in Mexico. Still another risk faced by companies operating internationally is that associated with transacting business in more than one currency.

A U.S. company with only domestic operations is accustomed to contracting all transactions in U.S. dollars. If the company creates a subsidiary in Mexico, its transactions will be denominated in at least two currencies, the dollar and the peso. As a consequence, the company quite likely will experience foreign currency gains or losses over time as the peso value fluctuates against that of the dollar.

Various combinations of events can create foreign currency gains or losses. The purpose of this chapter is to make the reader aware of the foreign currency exposure problem. This is accomplished first by discussing the basic causes of exchange rate fluctuations between currencies and by providing a brief history of the peso-dollar exchange rate. Also discussed is hedging, which is a method of reducing foreign exchange risk. Finally, a brief explanation of how foreign currency gains or losses are accounted for and reported on financial statements is included.

CAUSES OF EXCHANGE RATE FLUCTUATIONS

Prior to 1972, most countries pegged their currency to the value of gold—using the so-called gold standard. After 1972, the international currency market was set by supply and demand. That is, the value of currencies was allowed to float in the market, irrespective of the value of gold.

Under a valuation system set by the market, the values of different currencies change minute by minute relative to one another. Central governments can support their currencies in various ways, but in the long run, floating exchange rates are set by supply and demand.

Therefore, currency is similar to a commodity. The supply and demand for currency is affected by various economic and market factors. For example, a factor affecting supply is the rate at which the central government prints the currency; a factor affecting demand is the perceived strength of the currency.

Numerous other variables come into play as well. The inflation rate within a country, interest rates, balance of payments, government monetary and fiscal policy, and international perception of the country's economic and political condition all affect currency exchange rates. Obviously, these variables are all interrelated.

Understanding the causes of exchange rate fluctuations is a very complex task. Certainly, perfect knowledge of the causes of exchange rate changes would produce riches, as one could predict with certainty what would occur in the future. Since currencies are bought and sold as commodities, speculators abound in currency markets just as in stock markets.

Although we do not recommend speculating in currency markets, a brief investigation of the way professionals attempt to predict exchange rate shifts can be useful to understanding better the basis for exchange rate changes. Since exchange rate fluctuations can have adverse effects, it is a good idea to develop at least a basic knowledge of what could cause exchange rate variations.

Purchasing Power Parity

Purchasing power parity is a theory often used to explain, at least in part, why foreign currency values vary relative to one another over time. In theory, the same basket of goods in Mexico should have the same economic cost as in the United States. For example, assume a trip to the grocery store in the United States to buy a dozen eggs, a pound of butter, a gallon of milk, and a loaf of bread results in a grocery bill of $5. The same basket of goods in Mexico should cost the equivalent of U.S. $5 dollars. If the exchange rate is 2 pesos to $1, the basket of goods should cost 10 pesos if purchasing power parity exists between the two currencies. This example assumes away complicating effects of duties, import tariffs, and so on.

This simplistic example can be continued to illustrate one of the causes of exchange rate changes. If the inflation rate in Mexico is higher than in the United States, prices for the same basket of goods in peso terms will change more than in the United States. Assuming no inflation in the United States and 20 percent inflation in Mexico, the same basket of goods in Mexico would now cost about 12 pesos. But with no inflation in the United States, the price would still be about $5. To maintain equilibrium between the two currencies, a dollar should now buy more pesos. The predicted exchange rate would now be 2.40 pesos to $1. This is because $5 should buy 12 pesos under the theory of purchasing power parity (12 pesos divided by $5 = 2.40).

IMPLICATIONS OF EXCHANGE RATE CHANGES

The implications of exchange rate changes are more than academic. A few hypothetical examples will make the point.

Assume USA Company transfers $1,000,000 to Mexico to begin operations through the use of a wholly owned Mexican subsidiary, MEXCO. Further assume that the $1,000,000 is converted to pesos at the exchange rate in effect at the date of transfer, that is, 8 pesos to $1. MEXCO would have 8,000,000 pesos. If MEXCO subsequently buys equipment and buildings in Mexico to prepare to begin operations and the exchange rate changes to 10 pesos to $1, notice the assumed effects.

If MEXCO were to liquidate the assets bought in Mexico at the purchase price (no loss or gain on the sale) and convert the pesos to dollars, the resulting loss will be $200,000! Recall that the original investment of $1,000,000 purchased 8,000,000 pesos. If MEXCO takes the original 8,000,000 pesos and converts them to dollars after the exchange rate has changed to 10 to 1, the pesos will now buy only $800,000 (8,000,000 pesos divided by 10). The $200,000 loss is calculated by comparing the original investment of $1,000,000 to the $800,000 received.

Unless the conversion back to dollars is actually done, the loss is a "paper" loss. However, the paper loss will have economic effects. Furthermore, the loss must be accounted for, and this is discussed in the last section of this chapter.

Consider another example. Assume MEXCO borrows the equivalent of $1,000,000 in pesos when the exchange rate is 8 pesos to $1; MEXCO will owe 8,000,000 pesos. However, if the exchange rate changes to 10 pesos to $1, *in dollar terms,* MEXCO will now owe the equivalent of only $800,000 rather than $1,000,000.[1]

Obviously, the economic effects of exchange rate changes on an investor in dollar terms will be different depending upon whether the investor maintains a net asset or net liability position denominated in the foreign currency. The described effects are those which are reflected in the financial statements and are essentially indirect effects. What about more direct effects?

Assume MEXCO contracts with USA Company to import a particular product at $10 per unit. MEXCO operates in pesos, but USA Company will most likely want to be paid in dollars. If MEXCO signs a one-year contract to buy 10,000 units per month at $10 each, the total to be paid out equals $1,200,000. Assume an exchange rate of 8 pesos to $1 and the payment will require 9,600,000 pesos. MEXCO has used 9,600,000 pesos for planning purposes and has based the deal on this known amount. Notice what happens if the peso value weakens to 10 pesos to $1: MEXCO will now have to use 12,000,000 pesos to buy goods costing $1,200,000. In this example, MEXCO has to pay 2,400,000 pesos more than had been originally estimated.

One way to combat this problem is for MEXCO to maintain a dollar account in Mexico. Another way is to hedge, which is discussed in another section in this chapter.

Note that if the peso strengthens against the dollar in the last example, MEXCO benefits. For example, if the peso strengthens to 6 pesos to $1, MEXCO will spend only 7,200,000 pesos instead of 9,600,000.

Now consider the effect of exchange rate changes on MEXCO's competitive position in the international market. Assume the peso weakens against the dollar; it takes more pesos to buy one dollar. The converse is that the dollar buys more pesos. If MEXCO is exporting to the United States, MEXCO's product becomes less expensive in dollar terms and, therefore, easier to sell in the U.S. market. On the other hand, if the peso strengthens against the dollar, MEXCO's competitive position is weakened in the United States. A dollar will now buy fewer pesos, making Mexican products in the United States more expensive in dollar terms.

RECENT PESO-DOLLAR EXCHANGE RATE HISTORY

Studying recent history of the two currencies can provide a useful backdrop for understanding Mexico's general economic situation today. This understanding can assist in evaluating the future of the peso.

In the early 1980s, the Mexican economy became destabilized. Inflation began to increase rapidly, eventually reaching more than 100 percent per year. The peso, which had been relatively stable, began to devalue. Part of the reason that the peso lost value had to do with the Mexican government's campaign to nationalize industries, including banks. The government's philosophy caused a further weakening of the peso.

After being elected president, Miguel de la Madrid began a program to stabilize the economy and reprivatize industries. He was moderately successful.

President Carlos Salinas de Gotari took office in 1988. The peso valuation was reestablished at about 3 to U.S. $1 by issuing new currency known as the "new peso" (nuevo peso). Inflation was reduced to the low double digits and the Mexican economy appeared to be stabilized.

Ernesto Zedillo was elected president in 1994 and all appeared rosy. NAFTA was going into effect and trade with the United States was increasing as a result. However, it soon became apparent that the Mexican government had artificially supported the value of the peso. Almost overnight the exchange rate went from 3 pesos to U.S. $1 to the range of 7 to 8 to 1.

Many accusations were made about President Salinas's handling of the economy. Salinas's brother was indicted for murder and money laundering. The Chiapas unrest ignited international press attention. Inflation increased to around 50 percent. In the summer of 1998, the peso depreciated against the dollar again; over a one-month period the exchange rate went from about 8.5 to U.S. $1 to about 10 to 1. It remained in the 10 to 10.50 to 1 range for about 6 months. As a result, investor confidence weakened significantly.

The Zedillo administration has worked diligently to restore confidence. A bailout loan made to Mexico that was controversial in the United States was paid back early by the Mexican government. Inflation was reduced again to the 10 to 15 percent range by the middle of 1999. The exchange rate stabilized in the 9.20 to 9.50 range prior to the July 2000 presidential election.

The presidential election campaign during the spring and summer of 2000 was the most contentious in recent Mexican history. The PRI political party had held the presidency for over seventy years. Rumors were rampant about possible political and economic instability after the election. Both major candidates hinted that neither would recognize the election results if the other candidate won. As a consequence of this potential for destabilization, the peso weakened against the dollar, and the exchange rate rose to over 10 pesos to the dollar immediately before the election.

Vicente Fox of the PAN political party won the presidency, and the PRI did recognize the results. Subsequently, the peso returned to the 9.30 range as of the end of summer 2000.

Of course, many different scenarios are predicted for the future. Common wisdom in Mexico at this point is that the peso is somewhat overvalued and should depreciate against the dollar. Mexican citizens are acutely aware of the last devaluation that occurred right after former President Zedillo took office in December 1994.

President Fox assumed power in December 2000. However, no devaluation has occurred.

In our opinion, the election of Fox has resulted in a somewhat more positive economic sentiment, at least for the time being. Fox, a former businessman, was the CEO of Coca-Cola in Mexico and brings a businessperson's perspective to the presidency.

There has been discussion of linking the peso to the dollar.[2] Mexico already issues a type of short-term debt bond, called *tesobonos,* which is linked to the dollar.

An additional consideration in predicting peso valuations is the price of oil. Mexico has enormous oil and gas reserves. Reputedly, each U.S. dollar change in oil prices has a revenue effect on Mexico's income of U.S. $1 billion.[3] Therefore, a rise in oil prices should cause the peso to strengthen against the dollar, and vice versa.

The peso has continued to strengthen against the dollar through the mid-summer of 2001, ranging from 8.80 to 9.20. Most economists believe the relative strength of the peso is attributable to 2 factors. First, oil prices began rising in late 2000 and early 2001. Second, several Latin American countries, such as Argentina and Brazil, began to experience serious economic problems. As a result, many Latin American investors moved money to Mexico.

In summary, a benefit to doing business in Mexico for a U.S. parent company that establishes a plant in Mexico is the exchange rate stability of the dollar. This is because the parent, presumably, will be selling in the U.S. market and receiving revenues in dollars, and since the plant is located in Mexico, expenses will be paid in pesos.

There is a greater probability that the peso will weaken against the dollar over time rather than vice versa. The implications of this probability are twofold. First, if sales are quoted in dollars, the value of sales in dollar terms will not change. Second, if expenses are paid in pesos and the peso weakens, the expenses become "cheaper" in dollar terms. Therefore, net income should increase in real dollar terms.

Nevertheless, if the reader prefers to remove the risk from exchange rate fluctuations, there is a way. This is discussed in the next section.

HEDGING

Many companies involved in multinational transactions do not wish to leave themselves exposed to foreign currency exchange risk. Sales, purchases, and investments are made at a specified amount in a denominated currency, and uncertainty (and therefore risk) increases when the ultimate amount to be paid or received in dollar terms is not fixed. The future amount can be fixed in dollar terms through "hedging."

A hedge is a contract, in this case known as a forward exchange contract, that creates an obligation to deliver or a right to receive a specific currency in a specific amount as of a specific date in the future. For example, assume MEXCO is purchasing goods from a U.S. supplier at a specified price of $100,000. If MEXCO does not maintain a dollar account in Mexico, MEXCO could acquire a forward exchange contract to receive that amount on a particular future date in order to pay for the goods.

Although there is a transaction cost to the contract, similar to commissions paid for the purchase and sale of common stock, MEXCO has fixed the cost in peso terms based on the exchange rate in effect currently. It makes no difference if the peso strengthens or weakens against the dollar in the future; MEXCO has fixed the cost that it will pay based on what it had planned to pay.

Assume MEXCO sells to a Brazilian company and accepts a receivable from the Brazilian company denominated in reals. In this case, MEXCO may wish to fix the amount to be received in either dollar or peso terms through a forward exchange contract so that changes in exchange rates in the interim do not matter.

The idea behind hedging is to remove uncertainty associated with future exchange rate shifts. Although the contract has a cost, the benefit is the certain knowledge of the actual amount to be received or paid, fixed at the exchange rates in effect at the time of the contract.

EFFECTS OF EXCHANGE RATE CHANGES ON FINANCIAL STATEMENTS

Obviously, fluctuations in exchange rates can have economic effects. Often these economic effects are nothing more than paper gains or losses. Nevertheless, these effects must be accounted for in the financial statements. Recall the earlier example of USA Company forming a wholly owned subsidiary, MEXCO. USA Company transferred U.S. $1,000,000 to MEXCO when the conversion rate was 8 pesos to U.S. $1. As a consequence, MEXCO has 8,000,000 pesos. Assuming no other transactions and that the peso weakens against the dollar to 10 to 1, the resulting loss is $200,000; the 8,000,000 pesos are now only worth $800,000.

MEXCO's books are kept in pesos, so no record is made of the peso's weakening against the dollar. However, USA Company's financial statements are prepared in dollars. Accordingly, when MEXCO's financial statements are converted from pesos to dollars for inclusion in the consolidated statements, the $200,000 loss becomes evident. This is because, originally, $1,000,000 was transferred to MEXCO as USA Company's investment, and that investment is now worth only $800,000. This loss is called a foreign currency translation loss.

U.S. GAAP require that foreign currency translation gains or losses be accumulated and netted into one account. This account is reported in the equity section of the balance sheet.

SUMMARY

Dealing in more than one currency can add significant risk to business. Although dollar bank accounts can be maintained by corporate entities in Mexico, expenses are paid in pesos and the dollars must eventually be converted to pesos. When exchange rates vary, the timing of the conversion can create economic gains or losses.

Understanding the causes of exchange rate variations can assist in developing strategies to minimize the risk associated with cross-currency transactions. The theoretical economic causes of exchange rate fluctuations can be linked to differences in inflation and interest rates of Mexico and the United States. Inflation and interest rate changes within a country are driven by a complex set of factors. Exchange rates are also affected by intangible factors such as investor confidence in the government.

When buying or selling goods in another currency, the risk can be restricted through the use of hedging by buying or selling forward exchange contracts. Hedging has a cost.

Based on past history, the peso is more likely to weaken in value against the dollar than vice versa. This has beneficial implications for U.S. investors, especially if the Mexican operation has revenues in dollars and pays expenses in pesos.

Chapter 7

Management and Cultural Issues

Anyone who has managed employees knows that being an effective manager is a difficult task. Certainly all managers are keenly aware that each employee has his or her own personality, and getting the most from particular employees requires different strategies for each.

However, at least an American manager in an American company is managing within his or her own culture. Furthermore, that manager is managing employees who are predominately from U.S. culture. Although U.S. culture is not monolithic, the variations within the culture are relatively slight in terms of basic values that guide behavior with respect to the work environment.

What is meant by "culture"? Various definitions have been proffered. Culture is "the shared knowledge, beliefs, values, behaviors, and ways of thinking among members of a society."[1] It is "the collective mental programming of the people in an environment. Culture is not a characteristic of individuals; it encompasses a number of people who were conditioned by the same education and life experience."[2] One's personality and how one interacts with others, how one perceives events, and one's behavioral patterns are to a great extent influenced by the culture in which one grows up.[3]

The life experience of Mexicans is different from that of citizens of the United States. The difference in life experience between Americans[4] and Mexicans increases exponentially moving through the lower socioeconomic classes in Mexico.

Imagine how much more difficult it may be to manage in Mexico for an American. The initial impulse is to use U.S.-style management approaches. After all, such approaches have proved themselves by producing the most powerful economy in the world, and they can work in Mexico. However, they must be adapted somewhat to the cultural context.

As contact and interaction between Mexico and the United States have increased, the business culture gap has narrowed. This is especially true in the major industrialized areas of Mexico, such as Mexico City and Monterrey. Nevertheless, in any given company, the difference in business culture could be profound.

We acknowledge that, as we write about Mexican business culture, we are discussing generalities, and we caution the reader to keep this in mind. Neither the Mexican culture nor the U.S. culture is monolithic; variations exist in both. However, some general traits appear to be found in both cultures. The practical value of understanding these common traits is to gain insight on how to manage effectively in Mexico.

That is the purpose of this chapter, which will be accomplished by providing a theoretical background through reviewing research on cultural differences between Mexico and the United States. The theoretical background will provide the launching point for a discussion of cultural issues in practice.

RESEARCH ON CULTURAL DIFFERENCES BETWEEN MEXICO AND THE UNITED STATES

Academic research on the cultural differences between Mexico and the United States can provide a foundation for discussing specific issues and practical implications. Again, we emphasize that we are discussing generalities or propensities.

Perhaps the most well known and highly regarded research on cultural differences was done by Geert Hofstede.[5] Hofstede presented a questionnaire to thousands of employees of a U.S.-headquartered multinational company. The respondents were from forty different countries, one of which was Mexico. The cultural differences and similarities were grouped into four different classifications, defined as follows:

1. Power distance: the degree of acceptance of the unequal distribution of power within the society

2. Uncertainty avoidance: the ability of the inhabitants within a culture to tolerate uncertainty or ambiguity
3. Individualistic versus collectivist society: a social framework that is either loosely or tightly knit
4. Masculine versus feminine: the degree to which assertiveness, among other characteristics, dominates social interaction

Hofstede found that, in general, Americans prefer small power distances and Mexicans are comfortable with large power distances. Essentially, this implies that Americans believe inequalities should be minimized, that hierarchies are established for convenience, and that bosses should be accessible. Americans manage American companies based on these precepts about bosses and subordinates.

However, Mexicans view the relationship with their bosses differently, according to Hofstede's research. The Mexican culture has a tendency to accept large power distances. That is, in general, Mexicans believe that everyone has their place in an order of inequality. Bosses and subordinates each view the other as different types of people. Subordinates believe that their bosses are and should be inaccessible and that bosses have certain privileges by innate right. Furthermore, those in power should try to gain as much power as possible and look as powerful as possible.

According to Hofstede, Americans and Mexicans are also different in regard to the characteristic of uncertainty avoidance. Mexicans are more threatened than Americans by uncertain and ambiguous situations, and they struggle invariably to develop security in their lives. In this regard, they feel a need for written rules and place strong confidence in experts. They seek consensus.

Hofstede suggests that the combination of high power distance and strong uncertainty avoidance produces the desire for a powerful boss who can be praised or blamed. According to Hofstede, this situation satisfies a need to avoid uncertainty. If the inferences drawn are correct, obviously, a U.S.-style management approach employed in Mexico could have significant and potentially adverse implications.

The two cultures also appear to be different in relation to the individualistic versus collectivist cultural characteristics. The typical American is more individualistic than the typical Mexican. Collectivist societies place great emphasis on the family and on belonging to organizations. Friendships are determined by social relationships, with fewer crossovers between socioeconomic levels.

The one dimension in which the U.S. and Mexican cultures are similar is masculinity. Basically, men are expected to be assertive, and men's and women's roles are clearly differentiated.

Perhaps the most striking difference revealed in Hofstede's research is that of power distance. If Hofstede's conclusions are correct, participative management styles will not work in Mexico. To a great extent, what a manager accomplishes is based on the cultural conditioning of his or her subordinates. The implication is that U.S. managers will most likely have to become much more autocratic in their style to gain the respect of their subordinates.

Becoming more autocratic could negate popular management concepts such as empowerment. Hofstede opines that subordinates from large power distance cultures in countries such as Mexico would not appreciate decentralized decision making. All things equal, dependency needs in the Mexican culture push decisions as far up the organization ladder as they can go.

Other Studies

Results of a study based on in-depth personal interviews of Mexican and American executives in general support the findings of Hofstede. The interviews were analyzed for characteristics that could demonstrate cultural differences between Mexican and American managers. The characteristics of Mexican society and culture that were gleaned from the study are summarized here.[6]

Characteristic	Description
Family	Family is first priority; children sheltered; executive mobility limited.
Religion	Long Roman Catholic tradition; fatalistic outlook.
Education	Memorization; theoretical emphasis; rigid, broad curriculum.
Nationalism	Very nationalistic; proud of history and traditions; reluctant to settle outside of Mexico.

Characteristic	Description
Emotional sensitivity	Sensitive to differences of opinion; fear loss of face; shun confrontation.
Etiquette	Old-world formality; etiquette considered measure of breeding.
Grooming	Dress and grooming are status symbols.
Status	Title and position are more important than money in the eyes of society.
Aesthetics	Aesthetic side of life is important even at work.
Ethics	Truth tempered by need for diplomacy; truth is a relative concept.
Work/leisure	Work to live; leisure considered essential for a full life; money is for enjoying life.
Direction/delegation	Traditional managers autocratic; younger managers starting to delegate responsibility; subordinates used to being assigned tasks, not given authority.
Theory versus practice	Basically theoretical mind; practical implementation difficult.
Control	Still not fully accepted; sensitive to being "checked upon."
Competition	Avoid personal competition; favor harmony at work.
Training and development	Training highly theoretical; few structured programs.
Time	Relative concept; deadlines flexible.
Staffing	Family and friends favored because of trustworthiness; promotions based on loyalty to superior.
Loyalty	Most loyal to superior (person rather than organization); beginnings of self-loyalty.
Planning	Mostly short term.

Several other studies also shed some theoretical light on cultural differences. Many of these studies focus on the impact of family and group interaction in Mexico. One suggestion is that the work environment should produce an image of family, emphasizing teamwork and cooperation.[7] In this regard, the workplace should stress harmony, and sometimes performance pay can interrupt the social harmony of the workplace.[8] Nevertheless, when recognized and handled properly, cultural differences can be used to a company's advantage, if social networks are promoted in a way designed to improve productivity.[9]

CULTURAL ISSUES IN PRACTICE

Our experience is, to a great extent, consistent with the theoretical research on cultural differences between Mexicans and Americans. We have seen U.S.-style management philosophies used with success. In those instances, the common thread was an assertive, but communicative leader.

One caution that bears repeating and expanding is to remember that we are discussing generalities, and that different propensities exist in different regions of Mexico. It is the same in the United States; for example, Northerners have a somewhat different culture from Southerners.

The northern Mexican border is heavily populated with maquiladoras. Furthermore, due to easy access across the border and frequent contact between Mexicans and Americans in this region, U.S.-style management philosophies are probably better understood by Mexican employees in this area.

Mexico City is another region with considerable cross-cultural contact. Mexico City is a very cosmopolitan city, and executives of large companies, particularly, are familiar with U.S.-style approaches. As Mexico City becomes larger and more inhospitable, however, many executives and companies are leaving for other areas of Mexico, particularly central Mexico. These executives are helping to spread U.S. management practices, especially in Querétaro and Guadalajara.

The Monterrey region is characterized by heavy industrial operations. For example, it is the primary area within Mexico for steel fabrication. People from Monterrey are known for a strong work ethic.

The southeastern part of Mexico has experienced significant economic growth in recent years. Part of the reason is that Americans have overlooked this area in the past. As wages were bid up in other areas of the country, the Yucatán has become more attractive economically. People in this area are probably the least familiar with American business practices.

One final point about differences in general. Cultural differences within a country occur for socioeconomic reasons. In the

United States, for example, we know that a wealthy middle-aged businessman will exhibit somewhat different cultural characteristics than one of his middle-aged minimum wage employees. Nevertheless, the basis for those differences is relatively well understood in the United States. In Mexico, there are vast differences between socioeconomic levels. It would probably not occur to most American managers that some minimum wage earners in Mexico do not have electricity in their homes and therefore have no way of protecting perishable food. These individuals literally live day to day. Such an existence drives motivations and rationales in a way that would be totally foreign to a U.S. executive. Nevertheless, to run an effective operation, the manager should understand the bases for these very different thought processes.

This section includes a description of our experiences with specific cultural issues that could prove useful for understanding cultural implications in practice. The reader will note that the research on cultural differences previously discussed is conceptually congruent with our experience in most cases.

Executive Perquisites

Mexicans, both bosses and subordinates, are comfortable with the idea that rank has its privileges. Wealth and power often seem to imply a lifestyle that is privileged beyond what we would expect in the United States. For example, once while discussing a particular individual who was supposedly the owner of a business, a Mexican friend said, "He can't be the owner; he works there." However, in this case, the individual was indeed the owner of the business.

This incident illustrates two important points. First, the traditional view in Mexico is that owners do not actually have to work actively in their businesses. Second, philosophy and attitude are changing to embrace the idea that owners can be actively engaged in their businesses.

The following examples further illustrate the idea that rank does and should have privileges associated with it.

PRACTICAL EXAMPLE

At one plant, while discussing the time that the office staff was expected to arrive, the general manager of the plant responded, "I don't care as long as it is before me." The general manager indicated that he normally arrived between 8 and 10:30 a.m., even though production begins at 7 a.m. He also said that he did not need to spend much time there, as "the plant pretty well runs itself."

PRACTICAL EXAMPLE

After being contracted to assist a large company in Mexico City become more efficient, we noted that the top management usually arrived between 10 and 10:30 a.m. A sign at the back door entrances indicated the work hours and that the day began at 9 a.m. Each manager was taken separately to read the sign. When asked why they arrived late, each responded more or less the same—that the executives arrived late by custom.

One additional example concerning expected executive perquisites applies. Mexican managers sometimes have businesses "on the side." The supposed explanation is that salaries are low and it is expected that they supplement their income.

PRACTICAL EXAMPLE

A Mexican acquaintance was hired as a mid-level manager for a Fortune 500 company that has an office located in Mexico. The management team in this office was approximately one-half Mexican nationals and one-half Americans. The Mexican acquaintance was hired at the salary dictated by the local wage market; it was low by American standards.

Accordingly, the Mexican acquaintance began a business on the side. The other Mexican managers congratulated him on his initiative. The American managers were naturally displeased and told him that he must resign or give up his other business; they believed that he could not focus 100 percent of his effort with the company if he had another business. He resigned and went to work for a Mexican company that allowed him to keep his side business.

American companies want their managers devoting 100 percent of their workday to the company. If Mexican managers are hired, it may be wise to pay more than the Mexican market, if it is a depressed market, in return for the understanding that the employee will have no side businesses.

Titles

Titles are very important in Mexico, particularly in business. Using the appropriate title will assist you in gaining the respect of Mexican colleagues and subordinates.

People with college degrees use the title Licenciado(a), which is literally translated as "licensed." The title will appear abbreviated as Lic. on business cards and elsewhere. Mexicans refer to themselves and others by this title. For example, when on the telephone and asked, "Who is calling?" it is normal for the caller to identify himself or herself by this title, for example, "Licenciado Gomez." This may seem presumptuous to Americans, but it is the norm in Mexico.

The same is true for the professions. Engineers refer to themselves and are addressed as Ingeniero(a), abbreviated as Ing. Architects are addressed as Arquitecto(a), abbreviated as Arq. Accountants are addressed as Contador(a); the Mexican equivalent of a CPA is a contador público, which is abbreviated as CP.

It is common to address individuals simply by their titles alone, leaving off their names, for example, "Architect, how are you?"

A term of respect often used is Don or Doña for a male or female, respectively. This term is not always reserved exclusively for the wealthy or bosses. In some areas of the country, the term is used to refer to anyone to whom you wish to show respect. The term is used in conjunction with the individual's first name, for example, Don Roberto or Doña Maria.

Time and Patience

The concept of time is quite different for Mexicans and Americans. We are not discussing the stereotypical "mañana syndrome." Actually, the mañana syndrome is a sometimes-exaggerated problem. Punctuality, or rather lack thereof, is a stereotypical problem not so exaggerated. In social settings, arriving thirty minutes or more late is not considered late or rude. In business settings, punctuality is coming closer to American standards, but it still has a way to go.

One of the implications of the Mexican concept of time is that there is not always an appropriate sense of urgency. Employees should be given deadlines and convinced that these deadlines are not negotiable.

We have noticed that sometimes a seemingly intentional vagueness is mixed with a difference in the real meaning of verb tenses. For example, if a U.S. manager asked for a particular action to be accomplished, Americans would normally understand that they should begin the action. We have assumed the same understanding with Mexican employees only to discover later that this is not so. In some instances, an employee was asked to accomplish a task and responded "Yes." Upon checking we discovered that it was not done, and the employee replied, "What I meant was, I am *going* to do it." Our recommendation is to be very specific about expectations and time frames.

In almost every respect, time simply does not appear to be as important to Mexicans as it is to Americans. Time spent waiting in lines in Mexico is much greater than in the United States. The idea that waiting may inconvenience customers is not always considered.

Patience is truly a virtue in Mexico. Of course, patience and time are linked. If there is no sense of urgency, there is no need to

---

PRACTICAL EXAMPLE

In a retail store of a Fortune 500 company in Mexico, we were once shuffled between departments for an hour to obtain a proper factura. Then as the factura was being handwritten, the clerk received a phone call from another customer about the customer's account balance. We were kept waiting while the clerk attended to the caller. Meanwhile, three other clerks had nothing to do and were joking and chatting with one another. Even though we had stressed the extreme urgency of the task, no one was even apologetic.

be impatient. This seems to be especially true in negotiating and in establishing business relationships. Never be too eager to get to the "bottom line" of an issue; this is difficult for Americans, but it is important to keep in mind.

Planning

Mexican managers sometimes do not understand the benefits of planning. The implications of missing a deadline are sometimes not considered. However, our experience has been that when it is explained that American customers are demanding on-time shipments as a condition of sales, and the company is demanding on-time production as a condition of employment, the importance of planning is more easily recognized and embraced.

Planning is a type of control. Controls are management concepts that are not always well developed in Mexico. Sometimes Mexicans feel that they are "being checked upon" and take this personally. We have discovered that if an American manager adopts the role of a teacher and explains the "whys" of controls, checks, and balances that these concepts are more readily accepted. That is, emphasize that controls are designed to assist in the management process and apply to everyone across the board; controls are not meant to be personal.

In the past, many Mexican managers basically ignored strategic planning. One of the primary explanations is that the Mexican economy was subject to drastic changes over short periods. Another reason is that government regulations and tax laws are often changed without much notice, making long-term planning difficult. Nevertheless, strategic planning is an important aspect of management, and if the company is selling products to the United States, where the economic atmosphere is more stable, strategic planning must be done. Mexican managers can be helpful if the need for planning is explained and they are included in the process.

Negotiating

The affable warmth of Mexicans can be misleading when it comes to negotiating. They are tough negotiators; every deal seems to be negotiated as if it were a billion-dollar deal. They are also very patient.

A significant difference appears to exist between Americans and Mexicans in regard to fundamental negotiating philosophy. This philosophical difference can make negotiations difficult. In general, Americans take a comparatively long-term view, which implies the need for a win-win negotiated result. If the result of negotiations is win-lose, the losing party will constantly be on the lookout for an escape and the relationship will not last.

As discussed previously, Mexicans tend to take a short-term view. Perhaps because of this, they tend to favor negotiating results that are win-lose because, in the short run, they are able to gain more (assuming they are on the win side of the negotiations). This is consistent with the idea that the state of economic affairs is in constant flux and therefore one should take advantage of any opportunity to the greatest extent possible now.

Americans may begin negotiations assuming both sides are seeking a win-win result. This could be the case, but it might be a good strategy to attempt to educate the Mexican side about the long-run benefits of negotiating for a win-win result.

Opportunity Knocks

One of the implications to the ideas that the planning horizon is normally very short term and that the negotiating philosophy is often win-lose is that the situation may be viewed opportunistically from the Mexican perspective. The Mexican businessperson tends to squeeze the most possible from the existing conditions now, with no view toward the long run. If the Mexican businessperson senses vulnerablility, he or she is not likely to worry about what conditions may exist in the future or stop to consider the benefits of a long-term relationship. The goal will be to win today, irrespective of tomorrow's potential.

Economic Incentives

Economic incentives are certainly well understood at all socio-economic levels in Mexico. The lowest-level worker will figure out what is in his or her best interests, given the system that is put in place. However, because the economic situation of lower-paid employees is so terrible, by American standards, and because hope of escaping the plight is scarce, economic incentives are also viewed from a short-term perspective. There does not appear to be motivation to escape the plight, only to maintain it.

PRACTICAL EXAMPLE

The housekeeper of a friend asked for a wage increase. The increase was given and the housekeeper began coming only three days per week instead of the contracted five days. Since the housekeeper was paid on a daily basis, she was earning about the same as before. When asked why she was coming only three days a week, she responded that now that she made more money on a daily basis, she needed to work only three days.

Nevertheless, we and others have had success in finding those lower-paid workers who have a desire to learn and advance and in teaching them that they can improve their plight. Once they begin to improve their personal economic situation and advance, they become living examples to others.

Relationships

The old adage "It is not *what* you know but *who* you know" is much more apt for Mexico than the United States. Business and social circles are closely knit, and these networks are important.

Sometimes it is difficult to break into the business and social networks. For one thing, although Mexicans are an outgoing and affable people, they are suspicious—and for good reason. Mexicans are famous for looking for angles, as are all good business-people. However, Mexicans have raised "angle looking" to an art form that only the most clever and practiced Americans could achieve. Furthermore, from their perspective, Mexicans have many reasons to distrust Americans based on political history.[10] Therefore, Mexican businesspeople are naturally prone to suspicion and even more so when Americans are involved.

Since it is often whom one knows that is important, a good strategy to build relationships is to prove credibility through references that would be relevant to the Mexicans with whom one wishes to build relationships. Previous suppliers and/or customers may be helpful in supplying introductions. The U.S. Embassy or local consulate could also prove helpful, as well as international professional organizations or clubs.

Also keep in mind the importance of status and titles. One's own titles should be used in an almost flamboyant way as a method to help establish credibility. Never forget to recognize the titles and status of those with whom one wishes to develop relationships.

Certainly, using proper Mexican etiquette will be helpful. Finally, be patient in building the relationship.

Sí, No, and the Exact Facts

Mexicans work hard at being nonconfrontational and at keeping harmony. This is no doubt part of the reason Mexicans have a difficult time saying "no" outright.

Saving face is also important, even about trivial matters. We have come to believe that Mexicans as a rule do not wish to admit that they do not know something or that certain assigned tasks were, in fact, unfulfilled. Elaborate stories can be produced to explain why the outcome was different from what was expected.

Exaggerations and/or omissions of salient facts to mislead or just soften the effects of the actual facts are common. The following Practical Example portrays the flavor of our experience.

PRACTICAL EXAMPLE

An agribusiness client had been out of town for two weeks. He had acquired a herd of goats as an experiment to assist with weeding. In recent months, the goats had been dying mysteriously. When the client returned from his trip, he asked the foreman if any more goats had died. The answer was "No." The client, who is American, decided to count the goats himself and discovered that, despite the negative answer, one goat was missing. He returned to the foreman and proceeded to quiz him again. The foreman admitted that indeed one goat had died. When asked why he did not just say that to begin with, the foreman responded, "I did not think that you wanted to hear that any more goats had died."

In this case, "No" meant "Yes." In other cases "Sí" means "No." Experience is needed to become adept at understanding what is really being said. Keep in mind, however, that these distortions of fact are not usually done out of malice. In fact, in many cases, it is the opposite; they are to soften the effects of reality. Admittedly, this does not ease the effects of frustration. With teaching employees that management means having the facts, good or bad, the situation can be improved.

Artistic and Philosophical Nature

Mexicans are very artistic and philosophical; they appreciate art and they enjoy discussing philosophy. Most Mexican executives are well-read, have quick minds, and conceptualize very well. They are a romantic people, as well. The other side to this coin is that they are sometimes short on implementation and follow-through.

PRACTICAL EXAMPLE

The owner of a factory that made custom products for export to the United States was having difficulty satisfying his U.S. customers due to poor quality. Accordingly, he contracted with a Mexican national who was completely fluent in English to deal directly with the English-

(continued)

(continued)

speaking customers, translate specifications to factory workers, and be in charge of quality control.

This particular individual was very bright and well read. Focusing on quality control is mundane work. He preferred to develop elaborate marketing plans. Despite warnings to focus on quality control, the reason he was hired, he continued to exert most of his efforts on marketing plans. Eventually he was terminated.

In the same vein, form is sometimes preferred to substance and a "conceptual" solution is sometimes thought to be sufficient. In the previous example, the same executive thought the quality control problem was solved once he devised a series of elegant forms for use in quality control of production. Unfortunately, the forms were seldom used, but he believed the solution was the forms, rather than the implementation of a process that the forms were to document.

Family

Dependence on and loyalty to family are incredibly strong in Mexico. Normally, if forced to choose between family and work, family will be the choice.

Most Mexican subordinates accept orders from bosses with little or no critical thought; the order is to be carried out and the "why" is unimportant. It has been suggested that this is due to their upbringing, where family authority figures are omnipotent and omniscient. This sometimes results in employees who simply follow orders without thought of implications and if problems arise during the process, the process simply stops and the employees expect the boss to resolve the problems. American managers have voiced common complaints that once a problem arises, employees do not look for a resolution. Instead they go to the boss and expect the boss to resolve the problem, as opposed to taking personal initiative to solve the problem themselves.

One approach to defeat this tendency is to teach the concepts of empowerment. We have had mixed results with empowerment. Consistent with the cultural research, we have found that many mid- and most lower-level Mexican managers do not seek responsibility. In those cases in which the employee has accepted "ownership" in his or her job and taken responsibility for success or failure, the results have been positive, as one might expect. A collateral benefit is that the employee naturally understands the benefits of planning once he or she understands responsibility.

Etiquette/Courtesy

Mexicans are extremely courteous and respectful. Although most Mexicans understand that Americans are more informal, they also appreciate Americans who adapt to their culture. Mexicans are correctly proud of their heritage and culture, and showing respect for their culture is important.

PRACTICAL EXAMPLE

This story is typical of other stories we have heard from interviewing Mexican managers. In speaking with the Mexican managers of an American company, we learned that the Mexican managers had high regard for the American manager in charge of the office. It was evident that this was the case, and when asked why this was so, each manager responded more or less the same. The American manager had taken the trouble to learn Spanish and had adapted to the culture. The Mexicans were grateful that they had not had to adapt, but that the American had shown enough respect to adapt to them.

An easy way to show respect for Mexican culture is through greetings. Men who are friends normally greet one another with an abrazo. An abrazo is an embrace with a pat on the back that usually follows a handshake. It is an important sign of friendship but should only be used after establishing a good relationship.

It is very important to show the utmost respect for women. Americans are much more informal with women in a business setting than are Mexicans.

SOME FINAL THOUGHTS ON AMERICANS MANAGING IN MEXICO

Although the cultural differences are numerous and sometimes profound, many American managers can recount stories of success in applying U.S.-style management philosophies. An important element in these success stories is the presence of a strong leader who is also a good communicator. This seems to satisfy the condition of Hofstede's large power distance in Mexico and probably to some degree removes the uncertainty that Mexicans generally try to avoid.

However, strong leadership is probably not sufficient to manage in a truly effective manner. American managers should pay close attention to those cultural differences on which Mexicans place importance. From our own experience, we know that if American managers work hard at adapting to the Mexican culture, as opposed to demanding that Mexicans adapt to the American culture, they have a greater likelihood of success. That is, learning the language to make oneself understood is important, but fluency is not neccesary. Also, pay attention to Mexican mores that are embodied in etiquette and courtesy; respect the use of titles and so forth.

In those cases in which American-style management has not been successful, it is often because the basic participative American model has been used without adaptation. Mexicans sometimes interpret this model as being "soft" or showing weakness. Once this idea is implanted, the Mexican workforce will take advantage of the situation very quickly.

Never lose sight of the basic philosophical differences in a management context. In America, bosses have a tendency to embrace responsibility first and think about their rights as bosses second. In Mexico, it is often the opposite. Therefore, be prepared in advance to address this issue, as it will most likely arise.

Planning and organization are often less developed in Mexican managers. This becomes aggravated when there is no sense of urgency, which is a general tendency. In this regard, give consideration to teaching the concept of empowerment and empowering those managers who seem capable of embracing the concept. Once empowerment is embraced, the benefits of planning and organization are more likely to be understood.

In general there is a difference in attitude toward customer service. With regard to customer complaints, in America, the customer is always right; in Mexico, sometimes the attitude is that the customer is wrong. The basic philosophy supporting this attitude appears to be that the customer is seeking some angle from which to take advantage of the company, and in many cases that attitude is justified.

The good news to managing in Mexico is that Mexicans want to learn. This is half the battle. They also want to please. With the right mixture of cultural adaptation on the reader's part, teaching the "whys" of the processes, and firmness in management, the Mexican workforce can be very productive.

Chapter 8

Tax Implications for U.S. Citizens Working in Mexico

There are important tax benefits to working in Mexico. Knowledge of these benefits can be a very useful recruiting tool because, under certain circumstances, income can be earned tax free.

Most large companies are aware of these benefits and educate their employees about them. However, many smaller companies do not know or do not educate their employees about the tax benefits of working in Mexico. The purpose of this chapter is to provide basic tax information about U.S. tax laws related to U.S. citizens working in Mexico.

OVERVIEW

The U.S. government taxes worldwide income and requires U.S. citizens to file tax returns, regardless of where they are living and/or working. However, under certain circumstances, foreign earned income may be excluded from U.S. taxation.

Income subject to exclusion is graduated. For the tax year 2000, the amount subject to exclusion was $76,000. This amount increased to $78,000 for 2001, and will increase to $80,000 for 2002, and continue to increase in subsequent years. Beginning in 2008, the exclusion will be adjusted for inflation.

Income taxes paid in Mexico may be taken as a deduction or as a direct credit against U.S. taxes. A housing allowance may also be available for exclusion from U.S. taxes. It is not important where the employee is paid. That is, the salary can be paid in the United

States in dollars, even though the individual is physically located in Mexico.

These beneficial provisions were enacted by Congress to promote competition between U.S. multinational corporations. Often very high salaries are required to entice employees to move to foreign countries. Reducing or removing the income tax burden increases the effective after-tax salary. The result is that U.S. companies can send employees to foreign countries and pay lower salaries than would be required if the salaries were subject to U.S. income taxes.

SPECIFICS

To qualify for the exclusion of foreign earned income, an employee must have his or her "tax home" in Mexico. Tax home is defined as the country in which an employee is engaged to work. An employee's tax home may be in Mexico for tax purposes, even though he or she still maintains a home in the United States (see IRS Publication 54 for details).

In addition, the employee must meet one of the following requirements:

1. A bona fide resident of Mexico for an uninterrupted period that includes an entire tax year
2. Physically present in Mexico for a minimum of 330 days during any twelve-consecutive-month period

Furthermore, the income must be for services performed in Mexico, and the employee must expect the assignment to last at least a year.

To become a bona fide resident of Mexico as defined in the first requirement, the employee should apply for a resident visa, such as FM3. Furthermore, to qualify for tax purposes as a bona fide resident, the emloyee's residence in Mexico must be for at least one full tax year. For most taxpayers, this means from January 1 until December 31. For example, note that if a work assignment begins in December 1999, for purposes of this test, the employee must be a resident from January 1, 2000, through December 31, 2000, to become a bona fide resident for the year 2000; the employee would not be considered a bona fide resident for the year 1999.

After meeting the bona fide resident requirement for one complete year, the employee is thereafter considered a bona fide resident for every year or partial year he or she resides in the country. Continuing with the previous example, assume the employee left Mexico on July 1, 2001. For the tax year 2001, he or she is considered a bona fide resident due to previous qualification as such in the year 2000. Therefore, income earned in Mexico during 2001 is subject to exclusion.

The physical presence test in the second requirement does not insist that the 330 days be consecutive; however, it does require that the 330 days be "full." That is, travel days to and from the United States as well as physical presence in the United States count against the 330 days. However, travel to certain restricted countries, such as Cuba, would completely negate the foreign earned income exclusion. In calculating the 330 days, *any* 365-day period may be used.

PRACTICAL TIP

You are to be in Mexico on assignment for eighteen months but will not qualify under the first requirement. That is, you leave May 1, 2000, and the assignment will last until October 31, 2001. Furthermore, initially you will spend time traveling back and forth (twenty-one days) and you intend to spend fourteen days in the United States over Christmas. Toward the end of the assignment, you also expect to travel to the United States for another twenty-one days. Therefore, choose a twelve-month period that benefits you the most. In this case, assume from August 1, 2000, until July 31, 2001, you could meet the 330 full days requirement. Therefore, choose that period (August 1 through July 1) as the 365-day period, and the income earned during that period can be subject to exclusion.

Income taxes paid in Mexico are subject to a foreign tax credit or can be sued as a deduction against income on U.S. tax returns. However, the foreign tax credit is not available on income that is subject to exclusion on your U.S. tax return.

A housing allowance may also be excluded or deducted from U.S. income. This allowance is defined as reasonable expenses over a defined base amount for items such as rent and utilities. The base amount can be calculated using IRS tax Form 2555.

SUMMARY

Income earned in Mexico can be subject to exclusion from U.S. income taxes. The amount of income subject to exclusion is limited, and specific requirements must be met to take advantage of the income exclusion.

A little forethought and planning can go a long way toward maximizing tax benefits. Educating employees about the benefits can assist in recruiting those employees who might otherwise be reluctant to accept foreign assignments.

Appendix A

Selected Minimum Daily Wage Rates (Amounts in Pesos)

Mexico has a total of eighty-eight legally classified professions with daily wage rates by law based on economic region. Three such economic regions exist in Mexico: Area A is Mexico City and other regions in Mexico, Area B represents various different regions in Mexico, and Area C is primarily southern Mexico.

Profession	A	B	C
Auto mechanic	57.25	53.25	49.40
Bookkeeper	53.20	49.35	45.80
Bulldozer operator	58.10	53.85	50.05
Carpenter	55.00	51.10	47.40
Commercial cook	56.00	52.00	48.25
Electrician	53.90	50.15	46.55
File clerk	55.15	51.30	47.65
House painter	52.70	48.95	45.40
Professional nurse	62.45	57.85	53.80
Professional sewer	48.85	45.30	42.20
Plumber	52.85	49.15	45.60
Security guard	48.85	45.30	42.20
Welder	54.55	50.65	46.95

In Mexico, an employee is paid for seven days per week even though he or she may work only five days. Anything over forty-four hours per week is considered overtime. Furthermore, the previously listed selected wages do not include employer payroll taxes. The following example illustrates the calculation of the hourly cost to an employer for a professional sewer in Area C assuming a forty-hour workweek:

Daily minimum wage	42.20
Days per week	7
Weekly wages	295.40
Approx. payroll taxes due	40%
Cost to employe	413.56
Divided by weekly hours	40
Hourly cost to employer	10.34

Assume an exchange rate of 10 pesos to the dollar, and the approximate hourly wage is U.S. $1.03.

Appendix B

Spanish-English Glossary of Financial Terms

activo: Assets.

acconista: Stockholder.

acta constitutiva: Corporate charter.

administrador único: Single administraor. Mexicaon corporations are required to have either an administrator único or a consejo de adminstración.

aguinaldo: Legally required Christmas bonus; minimum of fifteen days' pay.

aportaciónes futuros aumentos de capital: The equivalent of other-contributed capital or capital in excess of par value. *See also* APORTACIÓNES PENDIENTES DE CAPITALIZAR.

aportaciónes pendientes de capitalizar: The equivalent other contributed capital or capital in excess of par value. *See also* APORTACIÓNES FUTUROS DE AUMENTOS CAPITAL.

asegurados: Workers who the hiring company has enrolled in social security; their salaries are tax deductible.

asociación en participación (AP): Joint venture.

auditor: Auditor.

balance general: Balance sheet.

bienes raíces: Real estate.

capital social: Legal capital of a corporation.

circulante: Refers to short-term, or current, as in short-term assets or debts.

comisario responsible para inspección y vigilancia: Commissioner responsible for inspections and vigilence; the equivalent of an auditor required by law to be appointed by the corporation.

compras: Purchases.

comprobante: Paperwork that proves an expenditure was made; could be a factura, nota, or recibo.

consejo de administración: Board of directors.

contabilidad: Accounting.

contador público: Certified public accountant.

corto plazo: Shortterm. *See also* CIRCULANTE.

cuentas por cobrar: Accounts receivable.

cuentas por pagar: Accounts payable.

deudas: Debts. *See also* PASIVOS, PRESTAMO.

diferido: Other, as in other long-term assets or other long-term liabilities.

dispensa: A basket of goods, such as toilet paper and canned goods, often given to employees as an extra benefit.

diverso: Miscellaneous.

efectivo: Cash.

egreso: Expenditure; an expenditure is classified as an asset or an expense.

equipo: Equipment.

escritura: The equivalent of a deed.

estado de resultados: Income statement.

estados financieros: Financial statements.

eventuales: Workers who are contracted but not enrolled in Social Security; their pay is not tax deductible.

factura: Legal invoice that must be used for assets or expenses to be considered valid for tax purposes.

fidecomiso: A bank trust used by foreigners to hold title to real property in the prohibited zone. The prohibited zone prohibits foreign ownership of real property within 50 kilometers of the coast or border of Mexico.

fijo: Fixed, as in fixed assets; also sometimes used for long-term, as in long-term debts.

finiquito: Government required severance pay when an employee resigns. *See also* LIQUIDACIÓN.

fondo fijo caja: Petty cash fund.

ganancias: Earnings. *See also* UTILIDADES.

gasto: Expense. *See also* EGRESO.

gastos prepagados: Prepaid expenses.

hipoteca: Mortgage.

Impuesto al Activo (IA): Asset tax.

Impuesto al Valor Agregado (IVA): Value-added tax.

Impuesto Especial Sobre Producción y Servicios (IEPS): Special tax on production and services.

Impuesto Sobre Automóviles Nuevos (ISA): Tax on new automobiles.

Impuestos sobre la renta (ISR): Income tax.

Impuesto Sobre Tenencia o Uso de Vehiculos (ISTUV): Tax on ownership or use of vehicles.

impuestos: Taxes.

ingreso: Revenue.

Instituto Mexicano de Seguro Social (IMSS): Mexican Institute of Social Security.

Instituto Nacíonal del Fondo de la Vivienda para las trabajadores (INFONAVIT): Fund for the National Institute of Housing for Workers.

inventario: Inventory.

inversión: Investment.

largo palazo: Long term. *See also* FIJO.

liquidación: Government-required severance pay when an employee is fired. *See also* FINIQUITO.

mano de obra: Labor.

materia prima: Raw material.

nómina: Payroll.

nota: Receipt for expenditures that is not considered valid for tax purposes.

notario público: An attorney with the power to file and record legal documents.

participación de los trabajadores (PTU): Participation of the workers. Profit sharing required by law that corporations pay to their workers.

pasivos: Liabilities. *See also* DEUDAS.

pedimento: Purchase order; when used in the context of import and export, it is normally used to refer to an official customs document; all temporary imports must be tracked and accounted for by this document.

pérdida(s): Net losses.

personas físicas: Tax term for individuals who receive taxable income.

personas morales: Tax term for corporations.

préstamo: Loan. *See also* DEUDAS, PASIVOS.

proveedores: Suppliers.

recibo: Receipt that is not valid for tax purposes.

Registro Federal de Contribuyentes (RFC): Federal tax ID number.

resultado de ejercicios anteriores: Retained earnings.

seguro: Insurance.

sistema de ahorro para el retiro (SAR): Savings system for retirement tax.

sociedad: Corporation; partnerships.

sociedad anónima (SA): Anonymous corporation.

sociedad anónima de capital variable (SA de CV): Anonymous corporation with variable capital.

sociedad civil (SC): General partnership used by professionals such as lawyers and accountants.

sociedad de responsabilidad limitada (SRL): Limited responsibility corporation.

sociedad en comandita: Limited liability partnership.

sociedad en nombre colectivo: General partnership.

sucursal de sociedad extranjera (S de SE): Branch of a foreign corporation.

sueldos: Salaries.

tesobonos: Short-term bonds issued by the Mexican government which are linked to the U.S. dollar.

utilidad: Net income.

utilidad bruta: Gross profit.

utilidades: Earnings. *See also* GANANCIAS.

ventas: Sales.

Appendix C

English-Spanish Glossary of Financial Terms

accounting: Contabilidad.

accounts payable: Cuentas por pagar.

accounts receivable: Cuentas por cobrar.

anonymous corporation: Sociedad anonima. (The technical term used by Hacienda for all corporations is personas morales.)

anonymous corporation with variable capital: Sociedad anónima de capital variable (SA de CV).

assets: Activo.

asset tax: Impuesto al activo (IA).

Auditor: Auditor. *See also* COMISARIO RESPONSIBLE PARA INSPEC-CIÓN Y VIGILANCIA, which is the equivalent of an auditor that is required by law to be appointed by corporations in Mexico.

balance sheet: Balance general.

board of directors: Consejo de administración.

branch of a foreign corporation: Sucursal de sociedad extranjera.

capital in excess of par value: Aportaciónes pendientes de capitalizar or aportaciónes futuros aumentos de capital.

cash: Efectivo.

certified public accountant: Contador público.

Christmas bonus: Aguinaldo; minimum of fifteen days' pay.

corporate charter: Acta constitutiva.

corporate taxpayers: Personas morales.

corporation: Sociedad; this term can be used also for partnerships.

current (as in current assets or liabilities): Circulante. *See also* SHORT-TERM.

debts: Deudas. *See also* LIABILITIES AND LOAN.

deed: Escritura.

earnings: Ganancias. *See also* PROFITS.

employees whose wages or salaries are not tax deductible: Eventuales. These employees are not registered with IMSS.

employees whose wages or salaries are tax deductible: Asegurados. These are employees who are registered with IMSS.

equipment: Equipo.

evidence of expenditure: Comprobante.

expenditure: Egreso; an expenditure may be classified as either an asset or an expense.

expense: Gasto.

federal tax ID number: Registro Federal de Contribuyentes (RFC).

financial statement: Estados Financieros.

fixed (as in fixed assets): Fijo; this term can also be used to identify long-term liabilities.

Fund for the National Institute of Housing for Workers: Instituto Nacíonal del Fondo de la Vivienda para las trabajadores (INFONAVIT).

general partnership: Sociedad en nombre collectivo.

gross profit: Utilidad bruta.

income statement: Estado de resultados.

income tax: Impuesto sobre la renta (ISR).

individual taxpayers: Personas físicas.

insurance: Seguro.

inventory: Inventario.

investment: Inversión.

invoice: Factura; a factura is a special type of formal invoice that is required to evidence an expenditure for tax purposes. *See also* NOTE AND RECEIPT.

labor: Mano de obra.

legal capital: Capital social.

liabilities: Pasivos. *See also* DEBTS.

limited liability partnership: Sociedad en comandita.

limited responsibility corporation: Sociedad de responsabilidad limitada (SRL).

loan: Préstamo. *See also* DEBTS.

long-term: Largo plazo. *See also* FIXED.

losses: Pérdidas.

Mexican Institute of Social Security: Instituto Mexicano de Social Seguridad.

miscellaneous: Diversos.

mortgage: Hipoteca.

net loss: Pérdida.

net profit (net income): Utilidad.

note (as in receipt): Nota. *See also* RECEIPT.

other (as in other long-term assets or other long-term liabilities): Diferido.

other-contributed capital: Aportaciónes pendientes de capitalizar or aportaciónes futuros aumentos de capital.

payroll: Nómina.

petty cash: Fondo fijo caja.

prepaid expenses: Gastos prepagados.

profit: Utilidad. *See also* NET PROFIT.

profit sharing (required by Mexican law): Participación de los trabajadores (PTU).

purchase order: Orden de compra. Note that pedimento can also mean purchase order, but pedimento is normally used in the context of reference to a customs document.

purchases: Compras.

raw material: Materia prima.

real estate: Bienes raíces.

receipt: Recibo. *See also* NOTE.

retained earnings: Resultado de ejercicios anteriores.

revenue: Ingreso.

salaries: Sueldos.

sales: Ventas.

savings system for retirement tax: Sistemo de ahorro para el retiro (SAR).

severance pay: Liquidación and finiquito are two types of government-required severance pay; the first is used when an employee is fired, and the second when an employee resigns.

short-term: Corto plazo. *See also* CURRENT.

sole administrator: Adminstrador único; one form of administration of corporations allowed by Mexican law; the other form is board of directors.

stockholder: Accionista.

suppliers: Proveedores.

taxes: Impuestos.

trust to hold real estate: Fidecomiso.

value-added tax: Impuesto al valor agregado (IVA).

Appendix D

Examples of Mexican Financial Statements

Chapter 3 illustrated the rigid approach to the application of tax laws. Mexican Generally Accepted Accounting Principles (GAAP) are similarly rigid in comparison to U.S. GAAP. The greater flexibility in interpretation of transactions under U.S. GAAP produces greater ability for creativity and for capturing the substantive economic effects of particular transactions.

The more rigid system that Mexico employs has certain advantages and disadvantages. Presumably, similar transactions will always be recorded in the same manner by all Mexican accountants. Sometimes, however, the substance of a transaction is different from its form. Under Mexican GAAP, this can create a problem in terms of capturing the economic essence of the transaction because form governs the recording of the transaction in Mexico.

Hofstede's study, discussed in Chapter 7, would predict that Mexicans want a rigid and codified accounting and tax system.[1] This prediction is based on the desire to avoid uncertainty and low scores for individuality for Mexicans, as revealed in Hofstede's study.

The Mexican Institute of Public Accountants is responsible for setting accounting standards in Mexico. If existing Mexican GAAP do not cover a particular issue, Mexican accountants are required to look for specific guidance through other formal standard-setting bodies, such as the International Accounting Standards Committee. That is, the options under Mexican GAAP are reduced by design.

The major difference between U.S. and Mexican GAAP is required inflation accounting. Accounting for inflation is required in Mexico due to the potential for distortion in the financial statements as a result of inflationary effects on the value of assets and liabilities. Since inflation has consistently been double-digit in Mexico, the purchasing power of the peso changes significantly over time. In other words, it takes significantly more pesos to buy similar assets now than in years past. Another example of inflationary effects is that revenues stated in pesos are worth less in terms of actual purchasing power now than previously. Inflation accounting adjusts the peso's purchasing power to a base year that equates current costs with the costs in base-year pesos to remove the effects of inflation.

From an analytical standpoint, inflation accounting can have a significant effect on standard profitability measures, such as return on assets and return on equity. The mechanics and calculation of the inflation adjustments are beyond the scope of our discussion. The net effects of the adjustments are to lower net income and to increase the recorded amounts for assets and equity. This will result in decreased profitability measures.

What follows are examples of financial statements for a small Mexican manufacturing company. The first set of financial statements is in Spanish, using pesos. The next set is in English, using dollars. For convenience, pesos were translated using an exchange rate of 10 to U.S. $1 and no adjustments were made for inflation and exchange rate gains or losses.

BALANCE GENERAL 30/06/2000	
ACTIVOS	
Circulante	
Fondo Fijo Caja	10,000 M. N. (Moneda Nacional)
Bancos	220,000
Cuentas por Cobrar	1,650,000
IVA Acreditable	800,000
Crédito al Salario	130,000

(continued)

(continued)

Funcionarios y Empleados	20,000
Inventarios de Materias Primas	220,000
Almacen de Refacciónes	17,000
TOTAL CIRCULANTE	3,067,000

FIJO

Maquinaria	1,450,000
Equipo de Oficina	280,000
Equipo de Fabricación[2]	308,000
Equipo de Transporte	450,000
Equipo de Cómputo	210,000
TOTAL FIJO	2,698,000

DIFERIDO

Impuestos Anticipados	10,000
Gastos Prepagados	204,000
TOTAL DIFERIDO	214,000
TOTAL DE ACTIVOS	5,979,000

PASIVOS

CIRCULANTE

Cuentas por Pagar	72,000
Impuestos por Pagar	501,000
TOTAL CIRCULANTE	573,000

CAPITAL

Capital Social	50,000
Aportaciónes Pendientes de Capitalizar	3,500,000
Resultado de Ejercicios Anteriores	560,000
Utilidad del Ejercicio	1,719,000
TOTAL CAPITAL	5,829,000
TOTAL DE PASIVOS Y CAPITAL	6,402,000

ESTADO DE RESULTADOS
Del 01/01/2000 al 30/06/2000

INGRESOS

Ingresos por Maquila	3,350,000 M. N.
Otros Ingresos	7,000
TOTAL INGRESOS	3,357,000

EGRESOS

Materiales Consumidos	8,000
Mano de Obra Directo	469,000
Gastos Indirectos de Fabricación	250,000
Gastos de Operación	850,000
Otros Gastos	61,000
TOTAL EGRESOS	1,638,000
UTILIDAD	1,719,000

BALANCE SHEET
JUNE 30, 2000

ASSETS

Current Assets

Petty Cash	1,000 U.S.$
Cash	22,000
Accounts Receivable	165,000
IVA Receivable	80,000
Government Salary Bonus Receivable	13,000
Officer Advances	2,000
Raw Material Inventory	22,000
Inventory of Machinery Parts	1,700
TOTAL CURRENT ASSETS	306,700

FIXED ASSETS

Machinery	145,000
Office Equipment	28,000

(continued)

Factory Equipment	30,800
Autos and Trucks	45,000
Computer Equipment	21,000
TOTAL FIXED ASSETS	269,800

OTHER ASSETS

Prepaid Taxes	1,000
Prepaid Expenses	20,400
TOTAL OTHER ASSETS	21,400

TOTAL ASSETS	597,900

LIABILITIES

CURRENT LIABILITIES

Accounts Payable	7,200 U.S.$
Taxes Payable	50,100
TOTAL CURRENT LIABILITES	57,300

CAPITAL

Legal Capital	5,000
Other-Contributed Capital	350,000
Retained Earnings	56,000
Current Earnings	171,900
TOTAL CAPITAL	582,900
TOTAL LIABILITIES AND CAPITAL	640,200

INCOME STATEMENT
FROM JANUARY 1 TO JUNE 30, 2000

REVENUES

Maquila Revenues	335,000 U.S.$
Other Revenue	700
TOTAL REVENUES	335,700

(continued)

(continued)

EXPENSES

Materials Used	800
Direct Labor	46,900
Factory Overhead	25,000
Operating Expenses	85,000
Other Expenses	6,100
TOTAL EXPENSES	163,800
NET INCOME	171,900

Appendix E

Useful Addresses

Mexican Consulates in the United States

ALBUQUERQUE, NM
401 5th Street, NW
87102
505-247-2147
FAX 505-842-9490

ATLANTA, GA
2600 Apple Valley Road
30319
404-266-2233
FAX 404-266-2309

AUSTIN, TX
200 E. 6th Street, Suite 200
78701
512-478-2866
FAX 512-478-8008

BOSTON, MA
20 Park Plaza, Suite 506
02116
617-426-4181
FAX 617-695-1957

BROWNSVILLE, TX
724 E. Elizabeth Street
78520
210-542-2051
FAX 210-542-7267

CALEXICO, CA
331 W. 2nd Street
92231
760-657-3863
FAX 760-357-6284

CHICAGO, IL
300 N. Michigan Ave., 2nd Floor
60601
312-855-1380
FAX 312-855-9257

CORPUS CHRISTI, TX
8800 N. Shoreline, 410 N. Tower
78401
512-822-3375
FAX 512-882-9234

DALLAS, TX
8855 Stemmons Freeway
75247
214-630-7341
FAX 214-630-3511

DEL RIO, TX
300 E. Losova
78840
830-774-5031
FAX 830-774-6497

DENVER, CO
48 Steele St.
80206
303-331-1867
FAX 303-830-2655

DETROIT, MI
600 Renaissance St. Suite 1510
48243
313-567-7713
FAX 313-567-7543

DOUGLAS, AZ
541 10th St.
85607
520-364-3107
FAX 520-364-1379

EAGLE PASS, TX
140 N. Adams St.
78852
830-773-9255
FAX 830-773-9397

EL PASO, TX
910 E. San Antonio
79901
915-533-3644
FAX 915-532-7163

FRESNO, CA
830 Van Ness Ave.
93721
209-233-3065
FAX 209-233-5638

HOUSTON, TX
10440 West Office St.
77042
713-339-4701
FAX 713-789-4060

LAREDO, TX
1612 Farragut St.
78040
956-723-6369
FAX 956-723-1741

LOS ANGELES, CA
2401 W. 6th
90057
213-351-6800
FAX 213-351-6844

MCALLEN, TX
600 South Broadway St.
78040
956-686-0243
FAX 956-686-4901

MIAMI, FL
1200 N.W. 78th Ave.
Suite 200
33126
305-716-4977
FAX 305-593-2758

MIDLAND, OH
511 W. Ohio St., 121
79701
915-687-2334
FAX 915-687-3952

NEW ORLEANS, LA
Bldg. 2, Canal St., Suite 840
70155
504-522-3596
FAX 504-525-2332

NEW YORK, NY
27 E. 39th St.
10016
212-217-6400

NOGALES, AZ
480 N. Grand Ave.
85621
520-287-2521
FAX 520-287-3175

ORLANDO, FL
823 E. Colonial Dr.
32803
407-894-0514
FAX 407-895-6140

OXNARD, CA
201 E. 4th St., Suite 206-A
93030
805-483-4684
FAX 805-385-3527

PHILADELPHIA, PA
Bourse Bldg., Ste. 1010
111 S. Independence Mall
19403
215-992-4262
FAX 215-923-7281

PHOENIX, AZ
1990 W. Camel Back Rd.
Ste. 110
85015
602-242-7398
FAX 602-242-2957

PORTLAND, OR
1234 Southwest Morrison
97205
503-274-1442
FAX 503-274-1540

SACRAMENTO, CA
716 J St./1010 8th St.
95827
916-441-3287
FAX 916-636-0625

SAINT LOUIS, MO
1015 Locust St., Ste. 992
63101
314-436-3065
FAX 314-436-2695

SALT LAKE CITY, UT
458 E. 200 South Salt
84111
801-521-8502
FAX 801-521-0534

SAN ANTONIO, TX
127 Navarro St.
78205
210-227-1085
FAX 210-227-1817

SAN BERNARDINO, CA
532 North D St.
92401
909-384-8113
FAX 909-889-8285

SAN DIEGO, CA
1549 India St.
92101
619-231-8414
FAX 619-231-4802

SAN FRANCISCO, CA
870 Market St., Ste. 528
94102
415-395-5554
FAX 415-392-3233

SAN JOSE, CA
380 North 1st St., Ste. 102
95122
408-298-5581
FAX 408-294-4506

SANTA ANA, CA
828 N. Broadway
92701
714-835-3069
FAX 714-835-3472

TUCSON, AZ
553 South Stone Ave.
85701
520-882-5595
FAX 520-882-8959

SEATTLE, WA
2132 3rd. Ave.
98121
206-448-8419
FAX 206-448-4771

WASHINGTON, DC
2827 16th St., NW
20009
202-736-1000
FAX 202-797-8458

Mexican Government Offices

Secretaría de Comercio y Fomento Industrial (SECOFI) [Department of Commerce]
Alfonso Reyes 30
Piso 10
Col. Hipodromo Condesa
Mexico, DF, Mexico 06179

Secretaría de Hacienda y Crédito Público (SHCP) [Mexican version of the IRS]
Palacio Nacional
Patio Central
Piso 3
Centro
Mexico, DF, Mexico 06066

Secretaría de Medio Ambiente, Recursos Naturales y Pesca (Semarnap) [Mexican equivalent of the EPA]
Anillo Pereferico Sur 4209
Piso 6
Col. Jardines en la Montana
Mexico, DF, Mexico 14210

Secretaría de Relaciónes Exteriores (Secretary of Foreign Affairs)
Ricardo Flores Magon 1
Piso 4
Col. Guerrero
Mexico, DF, Mexico 06995

Mexican National Chambers of Commerce

Camara Nacional de la Industria de la Transformacion (CANA-CINTRA) [National Chamber of Commerce for Manufacturers]
Av San Antonio 256
Col. Napoles
Mexico, DF, Mexico 03849

Confederacion Nacional de Camaras Industriales (CONCAMIN) [National Confederation of Industrial Chambers of Commerce]
Manuel Maria Contreras 133
Piso 2
Col. Cuauhtemoc
Mexico, DF, Mexico 06500

Confederacion de Camaras Nacionales de Comercio (CONCANACO) [Confederation of National Chambers of Commerce]
Balderas No. 144
Piso 3
Centro
Mexico, DF, Mexico 06079

There are many separate chambers of commerce for specific industries in Mexico. In the past, companies were required by law to join the appropriate chamber. Now, SECOFI requires membership in SIEM (Sistema de Información Empresarial Mexicano).

U.S. Chambers of Commerce

American Chamber of Commerce of Mexico
Lucerna 78, Col. Juarez
Mexico, DF, Mexico 06600
525-724-3800

United States –Mexico Chamber of Commerce
1726 M. St. NW
Suite 704
Washington, DC 20036
202-296-5198

U.S. Consulates in Mexico

MATAMOROS
Ave. Primera 2002 y Azaleas
Matamoros, Tamaulipas 87330
88-12-4402
FAX 88-12-2171

MÉRIDA
Paseo Montejo 453
Merida, Yucatan 97000
99-25-5011
FAX 99-25-6219

NOGALES
Calle San Jose s/n
Fracc. Alamos
Nogales, Sonora 84065
631-3-4820
FAX 631-3-4652

NUEVO LAREDO
Allende 3330
Col. Jardin Tamaulipas 88 2 60
87-14-0512
FAX 87-14-7984

The U. S. government maintains the following "consular agents" in Mexico:

ACAPULCO
Hotel Acapulco Continental
Costera M. Aleman 121
Office 14
Acapulco, Guerrero 39580
74-81-1699
FAX 74-84-0300

CABO SAN LUCAS
Blvd. Marina y Pedregal #1
Office 3
Cabo San Lucas, B.C.S.
11-43-3566

CANCÚN
Plaza Caracol Dos
2nd Floor, No. 320-323
Blvd. Kukulkan, Km. 8.5
77500
98-83-2450
FAX 98-83-1373

COZUMEL
Villa Mar Mall
Office 8
Av Juarez 33
Cozumel, Quintana Roo 77600
98-72-4574
FAX 98-72-2339

IXTAPA
Office 9
Plaza Ambiente
Ixtapa, Zihuatanejo 40880
755-3-1108
FAX 755-4-6276

MAZATLÁN
Rodolfo T. Loaiza 202
Zona dorada
Mazatlan, Sinaloa 82110
69-16-5889

OAXACA
Macedonio Alcala 201
Office 206
Oaxaca, Oaxaca 68000
9-514-3054
FAX 9-516-2701

PUERTO VALLARTA
Vallarta Building
Plaza Zaragoza 166
Piso 2-18
Puerto Vallarta, Jalisco 48300
32-22-0069
FAX 32-23-0074

SAN LUIS POTOSÍ
Carranza 2076-41
Col. Polanco
San Luis Potosi, S.L.P. 78220
48-11-7802

SAN MIGUEL DE ALLENDE
Dr. Hernandez Macias 72
San Miguel de Allende,
Guanajuato
465-2-2357
FAX 465-2-1588

U.S. Embassy in Mexico

Paseo de la Reforma No. 305
Col. Cuauhtemoc
Mexico, DF, Mexico 06500

Web Sites

American Chamber of Commerce in Mexico
<www.amcham.com.mx>

Mexico Connect
<www.mexconnect.com>

Mexico Online
<www.mexonline.com>

NAFTA (numerous sites, but start with this address)
<www.Mexico–trade.com/NAFTA.asp>

U.S. Department of Commerce
<www.doc.gov>

United States –Mexico Chamber of Commerce
<www.usmcoc.org>

Journals and Periodicals

Business Mexico
This is published by the American Chamber of Commerce in Mexico
<www.AMCHAM.com.mx>

Latin Trade
<www.latintrade.com>

MB: Magazine of the NAFTA Marketplace
<www.MexicoBusiness.com>

Latin CEO
<www.LatinCEO.com>

El Financiero
This is a *Wall Street Journal*-like periodical. The Spanish version is published five days per week. An English version is available in the United States and is published weekly.
<www.elfinanciero.com.mx> (Spanish)

Notes

Chapter 1

1. See A. T. Kearney's Global Business Policy Council's Foreign Direct Investment Confidence Index at <www.atkearney.com>.

2. *Maquiladoras* are discussed more fully in Chapter 2. A maquiladora is a Mexican corporation (possibly a subsidiary of a U.S. company) that imports raw material and equipment temporarily and duty-free for the purpose of assembling the raw materials.

3. <http://lanic.utexas.edu/cswht/tradeindex/index.htm>.

4. Maquila is a term used interchangeably with maquiladora.

Chapter 2

1. The Spanish terminology for NAFTA is Tratado de Libre Comercio (TLC), which is translated as Free Trade Treaty.

2. Maquila is also an antiquated term that refers to the amount of corn a farmer pays a miller for services rendered.

3. Branches of foreign companies may be established in Mexico after conforming to certain requirements. However, to be enrolled in the maquila program, the branch must still meet the same requirements as a subsidiary. Furthermore, companies may face adverse tax consequences when forming branches as opposed to separate corporations, which goes beyond the scope of this book.

4. The Harmonized System of Tariff Classification is used by the U.S. Customs Service and other countries to classify products into six-digit categories. To classify your product correctly requires technical knowledge. Your customs broker can provide this service.

Chapter 3

1. Inherent cultural traits may help to explain the rigidity in Mexican accounting and tax principles as compared to the United States. See Chapter 7 on cultural differences and especially page 125 of Appendix D.

Chapter 4

1. The corporate charter is referred to as *acta constitutiva* in Spanish legalese.

Chapter 5

1. The United States Census Bureau uses a ten digit classification system, while the harmonized tariff classification system (HS) uses six digits. The Census Bureau follows the HS but adds four digits to provide for a more detailed classification.

2. Lucentini, J., "Customs scrutinizes certificates of origin," *The Journal of Commerce,* February 9, 2000, p. 1.

3. Pedimento is technically translated as a "purchase order." The more common term for purchase order is *orden de compra.*

Chapter 6

1. In countries with high inflation rates and/or unstable currencies, loan agreements often contain provisions for inflationary adjustments that increase the nominal amount of the principal. This is sometimes true in Mexico.

2. Friedland, J., "Mexicans Quietly Mull Tying Peso to Dollar," *The Wall Street Journal,* September 28, 1998, p. A20.

3. Tricks, H., "Hurt by the Global Pinch," *Financial Times,* October 7, 1998, p. iii.

Chapter 7

1. Daft, R. L., *Management,* Third Edition, The Dryden Press, Orlando, Florida, 1994, p. 90.

2. Hofstede, G., "Motivation, Leadership and Organization: Do American Theories Apply Abroad?", *Organizational Dynamics, 9*(1), Summer, p. 43, 1980.

3. Berger, P.L. and Luckmann, T., *The Social Construction of Reality,* Doubleday and Company, Garden City, New York, 1967.

4. "Americans" in this chapter is a term meant to refer to U.S. citizens. Mexican citizens sometimes point out that they are also "Americans" by virtue of living in North America.

5. Hofstede, G., *Culture's Consequences: International Differences in Work-Related Values,* Sage, Newbury Park, CA, 1980.

6. Kras, E.S., *Management in Two Cultures,* Revised Edition, Intercultural Press, Inc., Yarmouth, Maine, pp. 68-73, 1995.

7. De Forest, M. E., "Thinking of a Plant in Mexico?", *Academy of Management Executives, 8*(1), 1994, pp. 33-40.

8. Flynn, G., "HR in Mexico: What You Should Know," *Personnel Journal, 73*(7), 1994, pp. 33-44.

9. Ruffier, J. and Villvicencio, D., "Local Loyalties: A Hidden Asset," *UNESCO Courier,* April 1994, pp. 23-26.

10. The Mexican and American versions of certain historical events are not always consistent.

Appendix D

1. Gray, S. J., "Toward a Theory of Cultural Influence in the Development of Accounting Systems Internationally," *Abacus*, 24(1), 1988, pp. 1-15.

2. Note that when equipment of a maquiladora is temporarily imported from the United States, it is not recorded on the financial statements of the maquiladora. However, the cost of the equipment that is temporarily imported is included in the calculation for taxes under safe harbor rules.

Index

Page numbers followed by the letter "f" indicate a figure.